In memoriam William L. Garrison, 1924–2015

Oxford Shakespeare Topics

GENERAL EDITORS: LENA COWEN ORLIN, PETER HOLLAND AND STANLEY WELLS

Shakespeare and the Afterlife

JOHN S. GARRISON

OXFORD
UNIVERSITY PRESS

Great Clarendon Street, Oxford, OX2 6DP,
United Kingdom

Oxford University Press is a department of the University of Oxford.
It furthers the University's objective of excellence in research, scholarship,
and education by publishing worldwide. Oxford is a registered trade mark of
Oxford University Press in the UK and in certain other countries

First Edition published in 2018

Published in the United States of America by Oxford University Press
198 Madison Avenue, New York, NY 10016, United States of America

British Library Cataloguing in Publication Data
Data available

Library of Congress Control Number: 2018938239

ISBN 978–0–19–880109–2 (hbk.)
978–0–19–880110–8 (pbk.)

Preface

The idea for this book emerged from a course that I taught in 2016. Funded by a grant from the National Endowment from the Humanities, I developed a first-year seminar that looked at diverse depictions of the afterlife across cultures and across time periods. My students and I explored the enduring question "What happens after death?" by looking at a wide range of answers from Buddhist and Hindu ideas about reincarnation, to classical notions about spaces of forgetting, to Christian beliefs about bliss and torment, to neuroscientific findings about near-death experiences. And, of course, we read *Hamlet*. Throughout the course, what struck us was not just the range of beliefs *across* cultures, but also the range of beliefs *within* cultures. *Hamlet* proved no exception. Indeed, Shakespeare's England marked a time and a place where beliefs about what happened after death were anything but hegemonic.

The course ended with a discussion of Billy Collins' "The Afterlife" (1990). The poem informs us that, while we are brushing our teeth and preparing for sleep, the dead are "moving off in all imaginable directions, / each according to his own private belief."[1] Some people are joining a celestial choir, while others are being squeezed into the bodies of jaguars. Some are in a place that sounds a lot like The Eagles' "Hotel California," while the occasional classicist runs into Edith Hamilton and her three-headed dog in the underworld. The poem offers a sort of inventory of afterlives, and its punch line is that "everyone is right, as it turns out."[2] This resolution was, surprisingly, a concept that my students latched onto as very convincing. What is startling about Collins' conclusion (even if it is intended to be tongue-in-cheek) is the seeming impossibility that all the ideas could be true. Isn't there just one answer about what happens after death, even if none of the living know what that answer is? An inspiring group of undergraduates in the fall of 2016 were willing to suspend the beliefs with which they were raised—and indeed the belief that there had to be just one answer—for a deep dive into a sampling of the curious body of texts that comprise the literature of the afterlife.

I am grateful for the National Endowment for the Humanities for the funding that allowed me to think deeply about this enduring question and, in turn, to add value to my teaching and to my research. Without the support of that vital institution, I would not have been able to engage the students in that class so profoundly as we navigated representations in order to move from *surveying* different formulations of the afterlife to *theorizing how and why* humans formulate ideas about life after death. In turn, this research and the students' dedication helped me see the potential for a book project emerging from it all.

Even before I started planning the course's content and the questions it would pursue, I had been doing my own deep thinking about the afterlife. During the year prior to teaching the class, my father was coming to the end of a long period of hospice care in the house where I grew up. During that time, he and I had several conversations about what he envisioned happening to him after death. I had similar conversations with my mother—about both what she thought would happen and what that meant for her. She was deeply invested, for example, in the idea that my father would observe us all after he died and that she would see him again when she died. My parents had very different ideas from each other, as my father did not believe anything happened after death (aside from decomposition of the body and lots of family matters of the legal and financial variety, as well the publication of a revised edition of his book). And not only were my parents' ideas about the afterlife very different from each other's, but also those ideas were very different from the ones with which they had grown up.[3] I appreciate my parents' openness to these conversations. I am also grateful for the serendipity that my father published with Oxford University Press and, though he did not live long enough to know that I would write this volume, I like the notion that my publishing with the same press constitutes a connection between us, even after his death.

At different times, fellow scholars read draft versions of parts of this book or provided useful advice in conversation. These people include Emma Depledge, Dustin Dixon, Karla Erickson, Margaret Ferguson, Stephen Guy-Bray, David Orvis, Megan Herrold, Kristine Johansen, Brittany Larson, Russ Leo, Marissa Nicosia, Kyle Pivetti, Richard Rambuss, Vanessa Rapatz, Melissa Sanchez, Goran Stanivukovic,

Will Stockton, M. L. Stapleton, Lisa Starks, Kristine Steenbergh, Jan Frans van Dijkhuizen, and Liz Weckhurst. Linda Braus, Nicole Polglaze, and Chris Bates were especially helpful with assistance with details in the manuscript. Peter Holland, Lena Cowen Orlin, and Stanley Wells, as well as Eleanor Collins and Jacqueline Norton, were very helpful in shepherding this book into the Oxford Shakespeare Topics series. Several research archives also played roles in supporting this project, both by providing access to rich archival materials and by cultivating environments where I could exchange ideas with other scholars. I am grateful to the staff of the British Library, the Folger Shakespeare Library, the Harry Ransom Center at the University of Texas at Austin, and the Newberry Library. The latter two generously provided fellowship support for this book project.

Contents

List of Illustrations

Note on Texts

All quotations from Shakespeare's plays and poems are taken from *William Shakespeare: The Complete Works,* eds. Stanley Wells and Gary Taylor, 2nd edition (Oxford: Clarendon Press, 2005). Unless otherwise noted, all spelling and punctuation from early modern texts have been modernized.

Introduction

The Undiscovered Country

Anyone reading or teaching *Hamlet* must wrestle with the ghost. To begin our consideration of the complexity of depictions of the afterlife across Shakespeare's work, it is hard to imagine a better example (or a better starting point for this book) than the encounter between Hamlet and his father (Figure I.1). Students are drawn toward this figure, just as the prince is, as it seems to possess not only secrets about the machinations that led to the current state of Denmark's court but also information about a world beyond our own. A vexed figure who claims to be suffering in the afterlife, King Hamlet demands that his son remember and avenge him. The ghost incites the action of the play while simultaneously signifying an ambivalence that links to the inaction that grips the play's protagonist. This spirit also links to the world outside the play in intriguing ways, as it points to debates and ideas about the afterlife circulating in early modern England. The ghost of Hamlet's father suggests that he will dwell in Purgatory "Till the foul crimes done in my days of nature / Are burnt and purged away" (1.5.12–13). The early modern audience might find the allusion to this location where the dead could be purged of their sins in order to earn entry to heaven striking as this notion was largely associated with Catholic beliefs. In fact, the Protestant Reformation brought with it a revision of a variety of ideas about the afterlife, including disavowing the existence of Purgatory and even questioning whether hell was a place of endless torment. Some early modern English writers continued to argue for the existence of Purgatory, though, and thus the reference might register diversely among playgoers. Further, the presence of Purgatory stands out in a story that supposedly takes place in pagan Scandinavia. Indeed, the appearance of the father's ghost immediately raises a series of questions about what happens after death: Can the dead speak to the living? What is

Figure I.1. "Hamlet, Horatio, Marcellus, and the Ghost," Robert Thew (engraver), after Henry Fuseli (1796).

Reproduced by permission of the Folger Shakespeare Library.

the duty of the living to the dead? Could Purgatory exist? Is this ghost even real? How can we discern a demon from a ghost or even from a hallucination? Is this entity a figment of the imagination (as some production decisions might suggest) or a demon in disguise (as some early modern Protestants would argue to be true of all ghosts)?

Hamlet seems truly to believe the phantom to be his father, yet he later suggests that a reunion with the dead would be impossible, given that the afterlife is "The undiscovered country from whose bourn / No traveller returns" (3.1.81–2). How can we reconcile the earlier encounter with the father and the words of the famous soliloquy? The play raises another vexed point with the decision to bury Ophelia in consecrated ground. According to widely held beliefs in the early modern period, suicide should exclude one from God's grace and block access to heaven. Yet the "coroner's quest law" (5.1.22) that has deemed her worthy of Christian burial suggests that human judgment can seek to influence the fate of the soul after death. As we can see in these quick brushstrokes, closely tracing contemplations of the afterlife in *Hamlet* invokes evocative questions about the play and renders visible the work's early modern cultural context. The more we look at this play, the more we see the crucial role of the afterlife in driving its narrative and shaping the questions the play invites us to ask.

While a cursory survey might lead one to claim that "Shakespeare never attempted the subject of Heaven and Hell," this book will reveal that we find the subject across both the plays and the poems.[1] In fact, the terms "heaven" and "hell" appear 655 and 169 times, respectively, across Shakespeare's canon.[2] And while these words are sometimes used as euphemisms or exclamations, their frequency signals how the afterlife is very much on the minds of Shakespeare's characters and poetic speakers. While the Reformation insisted upon the elimination of several religious tenets, it did not excise ideas about the supernatural.[3] Elizabeth I's court magician John Dee reported speaking with the dead, and James I discussed ghosts in his treatise entitled *Demonology* (1599). Pursuing questions about the afterlife in Shakespeare's work not only illuminates larger strands of thought in early modern culture but also offers insights into individual characters and specific situations in the texts. A single character's imagined fate after death can help us gain insight into that living person's fears or desires in the real world. Shakespeare's depicted worlds do not solely incorporate the plights of the living and the mortal. Nearly one-third of his plays contain speaking roles for supernatural beings. Examining the afterlife will allow us to make claims about some of Shakespeare's fantastical characters, including ghosts, witches, and demons.

As we will see, characters imagine figurations of life after death that are at times Catholic, pagan, or Protestant. At other times, these visions are unrecognizable within the terms of a single, coherent theology. Depictions of the afterlife thus dovetail with David Scott Kastan's claim that Shakespeare delivers an experience outside of history, "the workings of his imagination are at least temporarily able to escape the constraints of the orthodoxies, even of the controversies, that defined his age."[4] In turn, the range of representations in Shakespeare's plays reflects divergent strands of belief—hard-held convictions or ones that might be coming in question—among his audience members. Steven Mullaney notes that "theatre is a form of embodied social thought," and thus he extends the work of performance theorists such as Richard Schechner and Victor Turner who have shown the reciprocal relationship between drama on the stage and drama within the social sphere.[5] Yet Mullaney also importantly underscores that this embodiment can offer a "far from harmonious and not always therapeutic way of thinking, by means of actual bodies on stage and in the audience, about the larger—and largely virtual—social body."[6] This especially holds true of the Reformation where, as Mullaney and other scholars compellingly have shown, the theater offered a space in which anxieties and debates could be presented and worked through by inviting groups to experience a world both immediate and fictional. We might imagine productions of Shakespeare's plays—and the experience of watching them—as offering contexts in which audience members could ask questions and identify conflicts, rather than offering spaces that reinforce a single, hegemonic vision.

Although we can recognize strands of early modern beliefs and debates about the afterlife in Shakespeare's work, it becomes increasingly clear that how a character imagines the afterlife is often deeply idiosyncratic, ultimately mirroring her or his concerns and desires in the living world. John Casey ultimately concludes from his expansive study of cross-cultural figurations of the afterlife that "it seems likely that beliefs about the afterlife have been a function of how we understand and value this present one."[7] Throughout this volume, we will find that Shakespeare meditates on this notion through his many characters who vividly pinpoint their current position in the world when they offer their expectations of what the next life may entail.

The question of what happens after death was a vital one in Shakespeare's time, as it is today. And, like today, the answers were by no means universally agreed upon. Early moderns held competing beliefs about the afterlife and about how earthly life affected one's fate after death. Beyond the specific questions tied to King Hamlet's ghost noted here previously, other questions circulated in Renaissance England. Was death akin to a sleep from which one did not wake until Judgment Day? Were sick bodies healed in heaven? What kind of body would one have in heaven in the first place? Did sinners experience physical or spiritual torment after death? Would an individual reunite with loved ones in the afterlife? Could the dead communicate with the world of the living? Could the living affect the state of souls after death? The diversity of answers to these questions across Shakespeare's work can be surprising.

When we zero-in upon mentions of the afterlife in Shakespeare's work, we often encounter opportunities to explore new interpretations of the texts. Consider, for example, when Antipholus of Syracuse encounters the confusion within the city of Ephesus and asks, "Am I in earth, in heaven, or in hell?" (2.2.215). What does it say about the character that he cannot distinguish between the three? What does it say about the play's setting? Is the living world of *The Comedy of Errors* supposed to mirror divine forms of bliss and torment? Here and elsewhere, we find that the terrain of the afterlife sometimes functions to throw into relief aspects of situations in the living world. In *As You Like It*, we are told that "Then is there mirth in heaven / When earthly things made even / Atone together" (5.4.106–8). Why would those that populate the afterlife be invested in outcomes of conflicts in the living world? Who specifically are the absent, deceased characters who would care deeply about the outcome of events? How might the events of the play be spurred by their absence? In *The Tempest*, Ferdinand cries, "Hell is empty, / And all the devils are here" (1.2.215–16). Is this telling us something about his own expected fate after death, or is there something about Prospero's island that renders the boundaries between heaven, hell, and earth permeable? And how could one discern the divine from the demonic? In *Othello*, Iago relishes in the breakdown of such categories as he remarks, "Divinity of hell! / When devils will the blackest sins put on, / They do suggest at first with heavenly shows" (3.1.341–3). How could one ensure entrance to heaven? In *Henry VI, Part II*, Saye remarks that "knowledge" is "the wing wherewith we fly to heaven" (4.7.73). Is this simply his attempt to justify the large gifts he has made to "learnèd clerks" (4.7.70), or do we hear Shakespeare affirming the humanist education? Indeed, is it an echo of humanism or a more evocative statement about the afterlife when we confront characters' many references to the classical afterlife? And those references, too, are multivalent. For example, it offers a kind of comfort to know that Sebastian's soul resides in "Elysium" (1.2.4) in *Twelfth Night* yet Clarence's invocation of the "sour ferryman" (1.4.46) in *Richard III* suggests that his deceased relative experiences no such peace in what sounds like a journey across the River Styx into the classical underworld.

Whatever our own personal beliefs about whether an afterlife exists or what it might be like, we surely can recognize the powerful hold that loss and reunion have on our private emotions and collective consciousness. The familiar emotional tug we feel when we miss someone—whether a friend, spouse, lover, or family member—is perhaps largely why we fear death and why we mourn. When someone dies, we experience catastrophe in a way only hinted at by earlier partings. In Freud's terms, "normal mourning [...] overcomes the loss of the object while at the same time absorbing all the energies of the ego during the period of its existence."[8] In other words, we understand the people and things we love as extensions of ourselves. So, losing them involves losing a part of what makes us *us*, and we need to work through a process of reconstitution before we feel whole again. As David Eng and David Kazanjian have recently remarked, "as soon as the question 'What is lost?' is posed, it invariably slips into the question 'What remains?'"[9] The dead haunt the living in our memory, as we see reminders of the deceased in everyday encounters with architecture, images, objects, and even our own reflections in the mirror. Part of recovering from the death of another being involves resituating ourselves in a changed world. Jacques Derrida sees such a process as an active one and hence terms it "the work of mourning."[10] A confrontation with death triggers contemplations that change one's self and one's relation to the world.

Shakespeare portrays a broad range of "remains" that linger in the world after the living have departed. Mullaney's broader claim about early moderns holds true for the characters that traffic the stage: "feeling for the dead was still embedded and distributed across the sensible world, in names on gravestones, in the graves themselves, in monuments, portraits, biographies, and so many more private and personal ways, like the lingering smell of a father or mother or dear friend in a shirt or jacket or shawl bequeathed in a will."[11] Even in the absence of a ghost portrayed by an actor on stage, several of Shakespeare's characters are haunted by the palpable presence of those who have died. For Portia, the shadow of her father continues in the form of the casket challenge. Indeed, the very choice of the term "casket" for the boxes that enact her father's "will" signals how the dead man's desires inhabit the world he left behind. The notion that the father should choose the man who will marry his daughter and that the daughter should naturally follow his desire finds forceful expression as a symbolic afterlife in *The Merchant of Venice.*[12] In *Twelfth Night*, Viola's twin brother haunts her as she goes it alone after being shipwrecked in Illyria, much in the same way that Olivia is haunted as she navigates a world made new by the lack of a brother and a father. The linkages between these two women are captured nicely in a scene from Tim Supple's 2003 film adaptation of the play. While Shakespeare's text gives little indication of how Olivia spends her days, the film depicts her in a darkened chapel admiring an old photograph of the brother, reviewing an inventory of his old possessions, and even imagining him keeping her company by playing a piano nearby. The way the scene is filmed emphasizes what Freud sees at the heart of mourning: "the loss of interest in the outside world—except as it recalls the deceased—the loss of ability to choose any new love-object."[13] The implication that Olivia believes that her brother's spirit still resides with her in the room signals the excessive nature of her mourning, something clearly implied in the original play, and instantiates Freud's notion of the pinnacle of mourning which "leads to a person turning away from reality and holding on to the object through a hallucinatory wish-psychosis."[14] In Supple's adaptation, the ring she gives to the messenger Cesario (Viola in disguise) had been her brother's ring, suggesting she has chosen this new love object in a natural step that Freud sees as marking the termination of the state of mourning, when a person "is able to replace the lost objects with objects that are, where possible, equally precious, or with still more precious new ones."[15]

Certainly, we see this mode of transition even in Shakespeare's original play. Olivia will redirect her emotional energies from mourning her lost brother to desiring Cesario and then later to loving Sebastian. Freud suggests that we complete the process of mourning when we transfer our affection from a lost beloved to a new, living individual. However, this is surely only part of the story of how we are affected by our relations with the dead. Judith Butler argues that while Freud "suggested that successful mourning meant being able to exchange one object for another [. . .] Perhaps, rather, one mourns when one accepts that by the loss one undergoes one will be changed, possibly forever."[16] We, in fact, do see this in the case of Olivia. Making herself ready for romantic love involves changing her own understanding about the worlds of the living and the dead. Questions about the afterlife lie at the center of an early interaction in the play between her and her fool, Feste:

FESTE Good madonna, why mournest thou?
OLIVIA Good fool, for my brother's death.
FESTE I think his soul is in hell, madonna.
OLIVIA I know his soul is in heaven, fool.
FESTE The more fool, madonna, to mourn for your brother's soul being in heaven. Take away the fool, gentlemen.

(1.5.62–8)

In order to recover from her brother's death, Olivia will have to acknowledge her own foolishness and also come to see heaven as a place where she should be happy to imagine her brother residing. It is no surprise, then, that Derrida describes the "work of mourning" as a form of "*tekhnè*," that ancient Greek term for making or self-making.[17] For Olivia, clarifying her relationship to her dead brother and his status in the afterlife is central to the process of her determining who she is as she remains in a world without him.

Methods and Approaches

In order to model strategies for interpreting the work of Shakespeare, this book draws upon a variety of critical approaches to open up interpretations of the texts. Throughout the volume, the discussion will focus on close reading as a tool for parsing and analyzing multiple dimensions of the texts' language. Chapters will consider how key moments might have been staged in the early modern theater, as well as how they have been staged recently. Details of performance, such as how a ghost is costumed or the direction from which the spirit enters or exits, can affect our interpretation of the spirit's intent and nature. The decoration of a tomb informs our understanding of how a character is regarded by the living. Different approaches to textual analysis, furthermore, will help us unpack the implications of choices in the plays and poems. A consideration of material culture helps inform how the glass held by the ghost of Banquo might be staged or how the statues of Romeo and Juliet might be considered in early modern culture. Memory studies help us understand how the treatment of the dead reflects personal and collective beliefs about how one's life should be spent. For instance, tombs where spouses, siblings, or same-sex friends were buried together not only represent an effort to remember them among the living but also a hope that they be reunited in the afterlife (even in the context of a religious culture that largely rejected the possibility of such reunions). In the example of the joint tomb, we can see where the study of gender and sexuality also has a role, as the vision of the afterlife is powered by romantic desire. This critical field also informs discussions of how immortality might be realized through one's children. Various other terms and concepts from critical theory are applied at several points in the volume. Theory can prove a particularly useful lens through which to study the afterlife, as the question of what happens after death confuses seemingly stable categories of living/dead, here/there, past/future, and others.

As described next, the chapters in *Shakespeare and the Afterlife* discuss works across the canon and offer diverse approaches to pursuing the book's theme. Keeping its broad readership in mind, the book will emphasize not only how a specific line of inquiry can offer insights into the plays and poems, but also how literary texts can help readers explore their own points of view on a complex question. This book does not intend to be an exhaustive study of the entirety of Shakespeare's work or of early modern eschatology. It does not examine every ghost in the plays or every mention of hell, heaven, or the classical underworld. Nor does it provide a comprehensive history of changing attitudes among Christians (and others) in early modern England. It does seek, however, to be expansive and to invoke a range of examples that are examined in varying depth in order to suggest further directions for study. It does build connections between the texts, trace the most important instances of discussion of the theme, offer a synthesis of significant scholarship, and bring new insights to the plays and poems. And I hope it will inspire much more study of this topic.

Chapter Organization

Shakespeare and the Afterlife is divided into five chapters, in addition to this introduction. The division of the chapters reflects different stages at which an individual might approach death and contemplate the afterlife. We will find that an array of depictions of the afterlife occur across Shakespeare's works, often informed by the character's individual concerns or the cultural context in which the narrative takes place. Each chapter begins by discussing the implications of a particular phase of relating to the afterlife. Then, the discussion progresses to analyze representations in specific texts. Each chapter closes with a sustained discussion of a single text, modeling how a deeper engagement (e.g., a conference-length essay or longer student research essay) might function. In taking this approach to each of the chapters, I hope the volume will provide a synthesis of previous research and a roadmap of key instances across texts. I also hope the volume will point to different lines of inquiry that might be pursued in the future.

Chapter 1 takes as its focus "Contemplating Death's Approach." Characters across the play genres—comedy, tragedy, history, and romance—as well as the poems at times consider what awaits them after death. Indeed, individuals in Shakespeare's work take seriously the early modern injunction "*memento mori*" ("remember that you will die") which appeared frequently in literary texts and in visual art (Figure I.2).

The chapter also explores how suicide offered some individuals a means by which they could choose the time they would die, even as it put them in a precarious position in terms of their fate after death. After an exploration of characters' expectations of the afterlife in several major plays, the chapter concludes with an elaborated discussion of Claudio's expectations regarding the afterlife in *Measure for Measure* as the character's uncertainty drives him to imagine several possible versions of the dwelling of the dead. Chapter 2, "At the Gateway to the Afterlife," considers the space of the tomb as a site where the living feel close to the dead. The liminality of the space, as one that simultaneously houses the deceased and offers a place for the living to say farewell, productively troubles the distinction between the living and the dead. The chapter ends with a discussion of Cleopatra's tomb as a site where death and eroticism intersect, as well as a place where one can attempt to rewrite one's own life narrative.

Chapter 3, "Dialogues with the Dead," considers the desire to connect with others once they have crossed the threshold of the afterlife. The discussion includes encounters with ghosts and the

Figure I.2 "Memento Mori = Remember to Die" (woodcut), 1640.
Reproduced by permission of the Folger Shakespeare Library.

disembodied voices of the dead, as well as contemplations of the meanings of the dead body. The chapter ends with a discussion of how spirits in *Macbeth* not only haunt the guilty living, but also signal disruptions in the normative flow of succession. Chapter 4, "Raising the Dead," explores instances where the dead come back to life. We see this seemingly occur quite literally, where deceased individuals do appear to be reanimated from the grave, and also metaphorically, where the terms of resurrection help make sense of the power of reunion and the influence of early authors. The chapter ends with a sustained discussion of Prospero's claims of resurrecting the dead in *The Tempest* and how this applies to his relationship to the classical poet Ovid.

Chapter 5, "Achieving Immortality," discusses the memorialization of the dead as a form of afterlife for individuals among the living. Shakespeare's work offers several strategies for cheating death, whether by achieving immortality through fame, by influencing others, or through recreating oneself in children. The chapter ends with a discussion of the sonnets and the ways that these poems by Shakespeare suggest that immortality might be achieved not only through having a child or being written about in a poem, but also through friendship.

By structuring the book according to the stages at which one might encounter the afterlife, rather than dividing the book into chapters divided by plays or by genre, *Shakespeare and the Afterlife* encourages readers to explore diverse representations within a single work or to look for connections across works. The structure of this book is by no means the only way to think about the role of the afterlife in the plays and poems. Indeed, the afterlife itself makes a variety of different kinds of appearances and is itself porous and resists strict definition.

1

Contemplating Death's Approach

Death is the stuff of drama. Tension arises both when a character believes that death is near and when we admit that death's arrival can be unexpectedly sudden. In *King Lear*, Gloucester memorably remarks that "As flies to wanton boys are we to th' gods; / They kill us for their sport" (4.1.37–8). It seems that, whatever the conditions of an individual's death, its place in the larger scheme of things might appear unknowable. However, Caesar tells us, "It seems to me most strange that men should fear, / Seeing that death, a necessary end, / Will come when it will come" (2.2.35–7). Such an outlook offers a way to read Gloucester's claim as reassuring rather than anxiety-producing. Yet an awareness of life's precariousness might urge individuals to turn to religious or supernatural explanations for the seeming randomness of death, as Gloucester does in his description of the attitudes of the gods. Francis Bacon observes that atheism thrives in "learned times, especially with peace and prosperity; for troubles and adversities do more bow men's minds to religion."[1] We see this certainly in Shakespeare's work, where crisis and uncertainty drive characters to contemplate their fates after death. And, perhaps too, personal or larger social troubles drove playgoers and readers to Shakespeare's work as a way to explore how to make sense of an uncertain world.

Shakespeare's characters often find themselves in situations that spur a consideration of imminent death, and at times this entails imagining what might come after death. For some characters, this involves startling language describing concretely what they expect to experience. For others, this means reconciling with the unknowable nature of the afterlife. Hamlet famously describes dying as a journey to an "undiscovered country" from which "no traveller returns" (3.1.81). This idea echoes sentiments expressed by John Donne in a 1630 sermon delivered just a few days before his own death. The speech, later described as his "own funeral sermon," expresses his certainty that "death shall be an entrance into everlasting life" yet makes clear that "the disposition and manner of our death [and] what kind of issue and transmigration we shall have out of this world" are known only to God.[2] At the same time, Donne suggests that "all periods and transitions in this life," beginning with the emergence from the womb, "are so many passages from death to death."[3] While these experiences could not grant profound foreknowledge of dying, they could at least provide a conceptual vocabulary for imagining what the transition out of the realm of the living might feel like. Martin Luther, like Donne, claimed that we cannot know what comes in the next life because it cannot be comprehended with our human mental capacities. Consequently, he says such truths "won't be made known to us until hereafter."[4]

As we will see next, particular situations drive Shakespeare's characters to picture what their fate might be after death, and at times these are particularly individualized visions. It seems as if characters continually assemble versions of the afterlife that make sense based on elements of the present moment. For those who might reject Donne's notion that the afterlife is wholly unknowable, it stands to reason that they would envision the afterlife as a version of the world they inhabit. For instance, Thomas More's 1522 treatise *The Four Last Things* suggests that

> our sin is painful and our virtue pleasant, how much is it then a more madness to take sinful pain in this world, that shall win us eternal pain in hell, rather than pleasant virtue in this world, that shall win us eternal pleasure in heaven.[5]

More sets up a mirrored relationship between the world of the living and the experience that awaits after death. He cautions readers to choose wisely how they behave as it will presage their placement in either hell or heaven. The passage is structured in such a way as if to underscore that the afterlife is a reflection or amplification of the mortal life. Whatever minor pain or pleasure we experience when we sin or act virtuously is a taste of what is in store for us after death.

If we begin to look for this in Shakespeare's plays and poems, we can in turn gain some insight into his characters.

The freedom with which Shakespeare's characters imagine life after death in highly varied terms need not suggest that Shakespeare was an atheist. In fact, while it might be tempting to try to trace Shakespeare's religious beliefs from scant biographical information and from language in the plays, we can never know what Shakespeare *actually* believed or felt about the afterlife. We know that he lived in England in a time when church service attendance was mandatory. Shakespeare's father John was fined in 1592 for not attending church services, as was Shakespeare's daughter Susanna in 1606. We have no record of William Shakespeare being fined for such behavior, however.[6] This, of course, does not mean that he attended church regularly. Some scholars have thought that he might have been Catholic, but certainly he would have been exposed to varying Christian practices and beliefs. For example, we have records that he lived in a Calvinist household within the Huguenot community in London.[7]

It might go too far to suggest, as George Santayana did over a century ago, that Shakespeare "chose nothing" in the choice between "Christianity and nothing."[8] Yet, Santayana's clarification of that statement does ring true, that Shakespeare "chose to leave his heroes and himself in the presence of life and of death with no other philosophy than that which the profane world can suggest and understand."[9] As they consider their own mortality and what fate might await them after death, Shakespeare's characters often look inward for answers. They draw upon their own desires or anxieties in order to imagine what awaits them, often seizing upon figurations that relate to larger issues at work in the world of the play. Cynthia Marshall, in her study of Shakespeare's attitudes toward death and the apocalypse, finds that "at certain points the plays differ in fairly radical ways from the orthodox Anglican notions of the last things."[10] In the context of eschatology, the "last things" refers to the end of an individual's life, as well as the end of the world and the end of time. In these last things, we can locate crucial flashpoints for understanding individual texts, characters, and language.

Picturing the afterlife for figures we encounter in literature can be an evocative exercise, and it can also be productive in terms of spurring us to new forms of analysis and insight. Eric S. Mallin's *Godless*

Shakespeare opens with such an injunction to its readers: "Imagine an unearthly afterlife for characters in Shakespeare's plays."[11] It is certainly tempting to guess (in a Christian context) which characters an early modern audience member would expect to end up in heaven or hell. Indeed, whose actions seem to earn them an eternity of misery or of bliss? When we imagine possible scenarios for afterlives outside of the confines of the Christian context, Mallin notes, the possibilities become even more evocative. What specific torments or delights would be appropriate for each character? Who might return from the dead and to what ends? We will not need to do too much imagining, however, because so many of Shakespeare's characters engage in their own.

Death as Sleep

Even if the nature of the afterlife could not be known, some early modern writers at least conjectured about what the transition between life and death might feel like. At times, Shakespearean characters liken the transition from life to the afterlife to falling asleep. In doing so, they echo ideas circulating at the time. Martin Luther, for example, describes the soul as sleeping during death until Judgment Day. Such a comparison might be comforting for some, as it counters the unknowability of the afterlife with the familiarity of a nightly, bodily experience. In one of his speeches that end *The Tempest*, Prospero reassures the group gathered around him that "our little life / Is rounded with a sleep" (4.1.157–8). Hamlet, too, seizes upon this idea yet stresses that the psychic experience of that deathly sleep remains a mystery. He wonders, "in that sleep of death what dreams may come" (3.1.68).[12] Even if death looks like a very long sleep, the prince cannot imagine what the mind will experience. Other writers in the Renaissance found comparisons between sleep and death to be evocative. For example, the speaker in John Donne's Elegy 2 ("To his Mistress Going to Bed") reflects on the appearance of his undressing lover at "bed time" and finds it easy to imagine her as among the dead:

> In such white robes heaven's angels used to be
> Received by men; thou angel bring'st with thee
> A heaven like Mahomet's Paradise; and though

Ill spirits walk in white, we easily know
By this these angels from an evil sprite,
They set our hairs, but these our flesh upright. (10, 18–23)[13]

Fantasizing that his beloved might be an angel or ghostly spirit does not generate fear. Instead, it gives him access to a fantasy where undressing for bed resembles the transition from bodily, living experience to the union of spirits characterized by the complete bliss of heaven: "As souls unbodied, bodies unclothed must be, / To taste whole joys" (34–5). Such a vision makes for a very appealing afterlife, especially for a poet such as Donne who was deeply interested in both the sensual world and the nature of the divine.

The notion of death as sleep had rich religious connotations, especially given some individuals' belief that the soul dwelled in the physical body as it waited to awaken on Judgment Day. Thus, nighttime prayer took on special meaning, as it rehearsed preparation for death and because of course one could die during the night. In her study of sleep in the early modern period, Sasha Handley finds that the "prospect of death subtly coloured bedtime routines within daily life, where habits of early rising were symbolically aligned with hopes of an early blessing on the day of resurrection."[14] Once more, the afterlife is imagined within the knowable terms that define lived experience. We hear echoes of this in Shakespeare's Sonnet 30, in which deceased friends lie hidden in "death's dateless night" (30.6). The souls of friends might be assumed to be sleeping in this night, but (unlike the speaker) they have no sense of how much time has passed as the slumbering souls inhabit eternity. This depiction dovetails with Martin Luther's supposition that because "we can't get beyond the visible and the physical, [n]o man's heart comprehends eternity."[15] The terms of sleep and waking could be reassuring for some. Note how Donne's Holy Sonnet 6 ("Death be Not Proud") ends with the couplet, "One short sleep past, we wake eternally, / And death shall be no more. Death, thou shalt die" (13–14).[16] The eternality of the soul makes death less frightening as the sleeper only waits for the world to catch up.

The idea that death resembles our familiar experience of sleep can be traced across Shakespeare's work. For example, Macbeth says of King Duncan, "After life's fitful fever he sleeps well" (3.2.25). The grave figures here as a place of peaceful rest and of recovery from the suffering that is life. In *Henry IV, Part II*, Prince Harry mistakes his father for dead when the king is merely sleeping:

> —My gracious lord! My father!—
> This sleep is sound indeed. This is a sleep
> That from this golden rigol hath divorced
> So many English kings. (4.3.165–8)

The tension that arises from this moment, as Hal's father will mistake his son's relief that his father can rest for glee that he can seize the crown, heightens the dramatic conflict between characters. At the same time, this instance offers a rehearsal for when the king *will* die. Given the insistence by many early modern writers that death and sleep share a close kinship, we should hesitate before thinking it odd that Hal could be mistaken so easily. Thomas More posited that "among all wise men of old it is agreed that sleep is the very image of death."[17] Perhaps sleep offered an analogue to the peaceful rest one might desire in death. Montaigne, for example, describes an accident where he almost dies and depicts himself at the horizon of a peaceful state. In his most famous soliloquy, Hamlet says,

> To die, to sleep—
> No more, and by a sleep to say we end
> The heartache and the thousand natural shocks
> That flesh is heir to—'tis a consummation
> Devoutly to be wished. (3.1.62–6)

At first, he seems to say that dying means to no longer sleep. But then we see that he claims that sleep—"that sleep of death"—will end the suffering of the mortal life (3.1.68). The "consummation" reminds us that sex and death are also inextricably linked, as we saw in Donne earlier.

As we will learn next, while the sleep metaphor appears in several places in Shakespeare's work, it is not a universally held belief among his characters. Indeed, nor was it universally believed by other writers in the Renaissance. Ludwig Lavater, for example, calls into question the idea that "the souls sleep until the day of last judgment [because] this assertion has no ground in holy scripture."[18]

Classical Underworlds

As discussed in the Introduction, not all of Shakespeare's characters envision an afterlife that reflects the destinations described in Christian theology. It would make sense that characters in plays with events occurring in ancient Greece and Rome would imagine themselves destined for the classical underworld. However, we hear references to this underworld in plays that take place in both pagan and Christian contexts in England. In a play with a pre-Christian setting yet strong Christian overtones, King Lear wakes and believes he is in the next life when he says, "You do me wrong to take me out o' th' grave" (4.6.38), and a subsequent reference to the "wheel of fire" (4.6.40) suggests that he believes he emerges into the afterlife imagined by the ancients. The image suggests an allusion to the myth of Ixion, who is punished by being bound to a wheel that spins endlessly in Tartarus. He receives this punishment for being ungrateful both to fellow humans and to the gods, and Lear's choice to connect himself to this figure suggests he deems his mistake to be ingratitude. The "wheel" also points to the infinite nature of his punishment and reinforces the idea at the center of a belief in an afterlife that "the infinite significance of the soul's choices is best understood as the *eternal* significance of those choices."[19] Like Viola, mentioned earlier, Julia in *Two Gentleman of Verona* uses the term "Elysium" to describe the sleep of a "blessèd soul." The early modern setting of that play, combined with the use of "blessèd," shows the ease with which classical terms for the afterlife slip into Christian contexts (2.7.38).

The depictions of these classical underworlds are startlingly "out of time" in at least two senses. First, they transport figures from an earlier epoch into a later one. Second, as will be discussed much more fully in Chapter 3, these figures' contemporaneous interaction with early modern individuals challenges the notion of a linear, homogeneous experience of time. Early modern English literature offers a fruitful focus for inquiries into this phenomenon, given the frequency with which classical texts and stories were translated or adapted by Renaissance writers, who seized upon them as powerful source material and as a shared conceptual language among readers. Christian apologists portrayed the tales as allegories or early iterations of biblical stories; mythographers positioned them as fables with deeper meanings and described gods as personifications; and poets and playwrights drew upon the myths of classical antiquity for their richly layered connotations. Additionally, writers saw them as a common lexicon that would be recognized by their audiences. Lynn Enterline has shown recently how we can hear resonances of the humanist classroom throughout Shakespeare's poetry and drama. It is perhaps no surprise that the mythological afterlife offered a framework for understanding the experience of death as "humanist schoolmasters claimed that their methods of teaching Latin grammar and rhetoric would turn boys into gentlemen, that the eloquence and wisdom garnered at schools would directly benefit the English commonwealth."[20] We can consider the early modern present as a hybrid and re-evaluate the implications of Frances Yates's claim that "the great forward movements of the Renaissance all derive their vigor, their emotional impulse, from looking backwards."[21]

Whether Christian, pagan, or otherwise, visions of impending torment are the stuff of high drama. Heaven is perhaps too peaceful and therefore difficult to imagine. As Luther says, "What pleasure is like in eternity we cannot imagine."[22] The classical underworld, too, may be most appealing when it involves the specialized tortures depicted in myth, rather than descriptions of the space as a general environment for lifeless forgetting.[23]

Is it easier to understand extreme forms of torture than the highest forms of pleasure?

At the Gates of Hell: *Macbeth*'s Porter

With all of its planning of murder, acts of murder, retribution for murder, and regret over murder, *Macbeth* might be best described as a long meditation on death and its aftermath. Shakespeare stages Scotland as a place populated by the dead, and in turn the play offers contemplation of what comes after death. The setting of the initial murders offers a site to contemplate the threshold between world of the living and that of the dead, as well as a locale for a character named only for his profession to fantasize that he already dwells in the afterlife.

After the murder of Duncan, Macduff and Lennox hammer on the door to the king's residence. A Porter wakes to answer but is still intoxicated from the night's revelry. As he makes his way to grant entry to the two men, we have one of the most comedic and the most morbid scenes in Shakespeare. The Porter imagines that he is charged with managing the doorway not to the king's residence but to hell itself, as he pictures himself greeting a progression of sinners. Filled with gallows humor, his self-talk transports the audience to the cusp between death and the afterlife. As a plot device, the performance allows playgoers a break from the serious horror of the grim murders that have just occurred. At the same time, the performance encourages playgoers to contemplate the fate of those who commit crimes, as well as the role of those involved in the punishment of sinners.

The Porter responds to his sleep's interruption by complaining, "If a man were porter / of hell-gate he should have old turning the key" (2.3.1–2). On one level, the lines deliver a joke about the knocking being loud enough to wake the dead. On another level, these lines initiate a fantasy where this common man can pretend to be a much more mythical doorkeeper. It is meta-theatrical as the character, already played by an actor, imagines himself acting as a character in a situation much more dramatic than those in his daily life. When he hears "knocking within," he begins to engage in an extended scenario where he pretends to greet sinners on their way to the underworld (s.d.). At first, it sounds like a very old knock-knock joke. He repeats "Knock, knock, knock" as he grumbles about his job and also calls our attention to the onomatopoetic qualities of the word before asking, "Who's there, i'th name of / Beelzebub?" (2.3.3–4). The question positions him as "deluded into regarding himself as a devil," as Glenn Wickham observes.[24] Yet we also recognize this question to indicate that he is a human fated to play the same role in the afterlife as he played in the living world. Ultimately, he fancies himself to be one step above those condemned to be tormented, as he can announce those arriving to the underworld.

The first person to whom he imagines allowing entry is a man who has committed suicide after incorrectly calculating how much money he might make from his crops:

> Here's a farmer that hanged himself on
> th'expectation of plenty. Come in time! Have napkins
> enough about you; here you'll sweat for't (2.3.3–6)

Why did he kill himself? Is it that the crops underperformed? Or is it that *too much* success leads to misery? Is it the sin of self-murder or is it the sin of greed that brings him to hell, where he will need "napkins" (a piece of cloth) to wipe his "sweat"? The farmer offers an intriguing example of how someone's death often provides a starting point for wondering about the person's inner life. Consider, for example, the parallels between the farmer and titular character of Edwin Arlingtonin Robinson's well-known poem "Richard Cory" (1897), which describes the unexpected suicide of a lavishly wealthy and consistently chipper man. Paul Simon and Art Garfunkel adapted the poem in their 1965 song of the same name where a factory worker wonders why a man known for his excessive wealth, charity, and party lifestyle could kill himself. Death, especially suicide, sparks our curiosities about motive and the inner lives of others.

Although the farmer might not be nobility, we can identify kinship between his story and the genre of tragedy. Aristotle names as one of the identifying characteristics of the genre situations where "one of those who stand in great repute and prosperity, like Oedipus and Thyestes: conspicuous men from families of that kind" experience suffering and downfall.[25] As this might hold true for the farmer, it surely holds true for Richard Cory and for Macbeth. The scene is also important in the Renaissance cultural context, where "the most important conviction that emerges from the early modern poetics of tragedy is that *pathos* is the one indispensable element of tragedy."[26] Audience members should prepare themselves to place their sympathy not with the protagonist of the play's titles but rather with the victims of his ambition. We can locate elements of Macbeth's character in this farmer, as the protagonist kills the king—and ensures his own death—in expectation of his own kingship. Indeed, on some level, the play is a cautionary tale about hurrying fate or being too ambitious.

When the Porter hears knocking once more, he narrates an encounter with a figure who might be familiar to audience members:

> Knock, knock. Who's there, in th'other devil's name? Faith, here's an equivocator that could swear in both the scales against either scale, who committed treason enough for God's sake, yet could not equivocate to heaven. O, come in, equivocator. (2.3.7–11)

An "equivocator" denotes someone who does not seem to take one side or another. The introduction of "treason" of course points to Macbeth's crime of killing his king. We can see other elements of Macbeth in this equivocator, both because he wavers with indecision at times and more directly because he will come "To doubt th'equivocation of the fiend, / That lies like truth" (5.5.41–2). His failings have been deeply human, as he could not discern lie from truth, and supernatural, as he seems to have listened to the devil. The equivocator on his way to hell would also have resonated with more recent events in Jacobean England. Henry Garnet, a Jesuit priest implicated in a plot to blow up the Houses of Parliament with gunpowder, had authored a treatise in support of Catholics who maintained their beliefs. He was associated with "equivocation," a form of Jesuit logic that allowed Catholics to lie about their beliefs under oath if it could save their life or the lives of fellow Catholics. This alleged Gunpowder Plot conspirator recently had been executed, and thus audiences might imagine this public figure actually going to hell.[27] Some scholars have speculated that *Macbeth* may have been performed on August 7, 1606 for an audience that included Queen Anne and that celebrated King James' squashing of the Gunpowder Plot conspirators.[28]

The Porter claims the ability to identify categories of those deserving eternal torment, yet he knows very little about the actual details for the place. In the aforementioned quotation, he cannot remember another demon's name aside from that of Beelzebub. The Porter, himself, has an ambiguous relation to the afterlife. He describes his drinking as "an equivocator with / lechery" because it may incite the desire to misbehave but renders him unable to act on those desires (2.3.30–1). One might wonder just how qualified he is to guard doors if he cannot name those to whom he reports or who he is charged to protect. At the end of the play, when Macbeth perceives his imminent defeat and doubts "th'equivocation of the fiend," his pronouncement nods backward to the Porter's interlude at the earlier point in the play. The fantasy of this character named only for his failed occupation maps the play's protagonist's own path to a fiery union with the devil. In this short scene, we see how the afterlife offers a powerful heuristic device; it gives us a formulation or framework for understanding the characters who occupy the world of the living.

The knocking continues, as does the Porter's monologue. In some productions, the actor might point to or address members of the audience. Breaking the "fourth wall" in this way can be played for laughs or can demonstrate the power dynamics of identifying someone else as a sinner and destined for a fiery afterlife. After this next "*Knock within*," the Porter tells us,

> Knock, knock, knock. Who's there? 'Faith, here's an
> English tailor come hither for stealing out of a French
> hose. Come in, tailor. Here you may roast your goose. (2.3.12–14)

"French hose" implies that the tailor may have used too much cloth or overcharged for tony fashion. This "goose" might signify the fancy food he could afford and might also be an instance of the early modern slang for prostitute.[29] The slang term could indicate that the tailor commercializes (false) beauty. With the final knocking, the game seems to have grown tiresome for this drunk and tired Porter:

> Knock, knock. Never at quiet. What are you?—But this
> place is too cold of hell. I'll devil-porter it no further.
> I had thought to have let in some of all professions
> that go the primrose way to th'everlasting bonfire. (2.3.15–18)

He's gone from being a "Porter" to a "devil-porter," perhaps indicating how the imagined work of escorting others into hell has tainted his soul. When he realizes he can't answer the question to himself, "What are you?", he realizes that he has exhausted his imagination. He is both an enabler of evil and an incompetent doorkeeper and storyteller. Indeed, his poor job at guarding the palace has allowed evil to enter this place. Ewan Fernie interprets the Porter's complaint about the place being "too cold for hell" to imply that "the world of *Macbeth* is not only different in kind but actually is worse than Hell, or at least worse than Hell as we have traditionally conceived it."[30] Indeed, this is only one variation of Shakespeare's many hells. At the end of this chapter, we will see how Claudio, in *Measure for Measure*, imagines that the afterlife (presumably hell, in his case) might be freezing cold.

The end of the Porter's speech marks this interlude as a cautionary tale. The Porter teases the series of professions he might have named, and we can imagine how this might have played out like a perversion of the prologue to Chaucer's *The Canterbury Tales.* The notion of the "primrose way" links to Shakespeare's use of a similar phrase in *Hamlet*, which the *Oxford English Dictionary* cites as the origin of the more familiar version of this phrase: "the primrose path." Ophelia reassures her brother:

> I shall th'effect of this good lesson keep
> As watchman to my heart; but, good my brother,
> Do not, as some ungracious pastors do,
> Show me the steep and thorny way to heaven
> Whilst like a puffed and reckless libertine
> Himself the primrose path of dalliance treads
> And recks not his own rede. (1.3.45–51)

The phrase "primrose path" has special meaning for Ophelia, who will eventually drown as she picks flowers by a stream. These lines in *Macbeth* and *Hamlet* have the same connotation. Taking the easy way can lead one to hell. This seems true of Macbeth, where hurrying his fortune and trying to avoid the work it would take to earn a place as king leads to committing the crime of murder and to his own quick demise. The way to heaven is "steep and thorny," as hard work is needed to reach a better afterlife. Neither Macbeth nor this Porter seem fit for such thoughtful and patient efforts.

Upon the final "*Knock within*," we finally have characters from the play pass through the Porter's gate. Macduff and Lennox enter. They, too, are on their way to hell, it would seem. And the Porter *has* actually been very close to the afterlife, as death is occurring nearby. The Porter's exclamation before greeting the two men, "Anon, anon! / I pray you remember the porter," implies that Macduff and Lenox might see the actual porter of hell soon (2.3.19–20). It also might be an injunction to the audience members, who have been the only witnesses of his little fantasy, to think of this little drama as a cautionary tale. We should note also that the phrase "remember the porter" has intriguing parallels to the words of Hamlet's father, who urges "remember me" as he exits after his dialogue with the prince. Both characters seem to have useful, if cryptic, information for the living based on their (real or imagined) intimacy with the afterlife.

The Deathbed Encounter in *Othello*

The deathbed represents a place and a time of transition from life to afterlife, often involving an audience for the final moments of a character's life. It is a fraught site, characterized by what Karla Erickson terms "dilemmas of the threshold" as the deathbed often operates as "an indeterminate state between actively living and actively dying."[31] An early seventeenth-century Puritan manuscript of a deathbed dialogue consoles a dying man this way:

> Brother my full persuasion is that your comfort will come at an Instant unexpected in such a season as shall be best for you & before you yet die, And this I ground upon experience of god's late dealing with me in a visitation of sickness near to death, when after an hard conflict for half a night one a sudden many sweet promises & [melting] in visitations of grace came to my thoughts upon which my heart was unspeakable joyful & comfortable and then nothing revived my spirit then the thought of death & the apprehension of my future glory at [hand]. (7r–7v)[32]

The afterlife here is soothing and offers a salve for the dying man who is physically suffering. Death revives his spirit, as dying is seen as the entry to a better life. In fact, we see such an attitude in Shakespeare's work, and it was a common one in the broader early modern culture. Note, for example, in *Henry VI, Part II* when the king looks upon the suffering Cardinal Beaufort and remarks, "Ah, what a sign it is of evil life / Where death's approach is seen so terrible" (3.3.5–6). This idea that one's deathbed experience predicts their destination after death finds expression in the history of reports of near-death experiences because, as Zaleski observes, "in otherworld journey literature, only those destined for hell [...] cling to life."[33] Yet this idea was not a universally held one. Donne, in his final sermon, warns against reading too much into the scene of a deathbed. He cautions against taking the condition or countenance of the dying as "presagition of spiritual death and damnation," noting that about one person's death it might "be testified that he went away like a lamb, that is, without any reluctation" while another's death might be "accompanied with a dangerous damp and stupefaction, and insensibility of his present state."[34] Consider, too, how Hamlet describes a commonly held "dread" experienced when we contemplate the afterlife, a locale "we know not of" (3.1.80; 3.1.84).

Figure 1.1. "The dying hour of the rich man from the parable of Lazarus and the rich man," Martin de Voss (between 1590 and 1610).

Courtesy of The Folger Shakespeare Library.

The differing strands of thought in Shakespeare's culture may have opened opportunities for his plays to stage provocative fictions. Indeed, a dying person's bedside might take on the quality of theater as it gathers an audience and performs various rituals (Figure 1.1.).

In the final scene of *Othello*, the protagonist imagines at Desdemona's deathbed that the two of them will reunite after death. After smothering her, he looks forward to "When we shall meet at count / This look of thine will hurl my soul from heaven, / and fiends will snatch at it. Cold, cold, my girl" (5.2.280–3). "Count" refers to Judgment Day and to the specific moment when his wife's soul will wake to judge Othello and ensure that he is cast out of heaven. His repetition of "cold" underscores that her presently cooling body predicts her future attitude toward him in the afterlife. He goes on:

> Whip me, ye devils,
> From the possession of this heavenly sight.

> Blow me about in winds, roast me in sulphur,
> Wash me in steep-down gulfs of liquid fire!
> O Desdemona! Dead Desdemona! Dead! O! O! (5.2.284–8)

Many early moderns imagined demons to be present in the room with the dying. And such entities would occupy a curious position in time. They are both the ones that the damned would encounter in the future and the ones that torture or tempt the dying in the *now*. The imagined demons also present a strange spatial ambiguity. Invisible to all but the dying, are they located in the afterlife or the world of the living? Kristin Poole suggests that the ending of *Othello* is in close dialogue with *ars moriendi* texts, which discussed the craft of dying and assumed the devil or demons to be present at the bedside of the dying. As she notes, "the interior space of the bedchamber is at once the scene of early modern domesticity and the traditional site of engagement with the supernatural, since the deathbed was perceived as a moment of combat between the dying person's soul and the devil."[35] Recognizing that Othello ensures that Desdemona has prayed and asks her to confess, Poole posits that Othello is "guiding her through the rituals of a good death, those intended to aid *Moriens* [the dying] against the devil's assault."[36] Othello's reference to Iago as a "demi-devil" and his suggestion that the schemer may have hooves suggests that this bedside miscreant may in fact be a demon (5.2.307; 5.2.292).

Othello does indeed seem concerned about Desdemona's state after death. He remarks about not harming the "monumental alabaster" of Desdemona's skin, which Ramie Targoff interprets to indicate "the equivalent of the marble effigy that will grace her tomb, preserving her beauty for posthumous veneration" (5.2.5).[37] His preservation of her beauty, combined with the way that the scene conflates erotic affection with murderous action, leaves us unable to disaggregate his love for her and his anger toward her. He says, "I kissed thee ere I killed thee," echoing a line from *Venus and Adonis*, in which the goddess of love "murders with a kiss" (5.2.368; 54). As the play's ending turns on the care with which Othello murders his beloved and his immediate regret, we can see Othello emerge as the tragic hero of the play. Before his suicide, Othello announces that he should be remembered as a fierce soldier who did service for the state. Cassio says of his friend's suicide, "This I did fear," and Lodovico describes his corpse beside Desdemona's as "the tragic loading of this bed" (5.2.370; 5.2.373). The scene opens the possibility of reading Othello's suicide both as the result of devilish manipulation and as an honorable death. As discussed next, he is one of many Shakespearean protagonists who take their own life and are valorized for it.

Suicide and the Fate of the Soul

One way to be certain of the hour of one's death and to hasten one's entry into the afterlife was to commit suicide. As Cassius reminds Casca in *Julius Caesar*, "life, being weary of these worldly bars, / Never lacks power to dismiss itself" (1.3.95–6). That is, one can always take one's own life. And, in the classical Roman setting of that play, suicide would not carry the connotation of sin that it would in the Christian context of Shakespeare's age. Othello commits suicide after realizing that he was manipulated into killing Desdemona. The question of whether taking one's own life damned the soul was a vexed one in early modern England. In addition to Othello, many other Shakespearean characters who commit suicide—including Cleopatra, Juliet, Lucrece, Ophelia, and Rome—are depicted sympathetically.

Like many suicides in Shakespeare, Cleopatra's is not treated with scorn. The queen follows "what's brave, what's noble, / [. . .] the high Roman fashion" (4.16.88–9) and is praised by Augustus Caesar as "Bravest at the last, / She levelled at our purposes, and, being royal, / Took her own way" (5.2.329–31). Instances of suicide further remind us that the nature of the afterlife may vary across works, given that characters from antiquity potentially saw taking one's life as an act of valor. Indeed, Cleopatra tells her court that suicide will "make death proud to take us" (4.16.90).[38] The valorization of her suicide partly can be explained by the temporal location of the play in pagan times. But we can also understand suicide as becoming an available object for writers, as some saw suicide as not necessarily charged with religious valences. In the early modern period, "self-killing lost its supernatural character—at least in the eyes of the upper and middling classes—and that change was one aspect of a wider growth of skepticism about the supernatural."[39] As Michael MacDonald and Terence R. Murphy have shown, early modern responses to suicide "first hardened and then grew more tolerant and sympathetic."[40] MacDonald and Murphy's study identifies the softening of attitudes toward suicide as occurring largely in the second half of the seventeenth century. However, their study also acknowledges literature's role in forming the foundation for changing attitudes. Citing *Hamlet*, they reflect upon how Shakespeare "presents the entire range of opinion about the legitimacy and morality of suicide."[41] After Lucrece's father and her husband passionately bewail her death, the instance becomes a moment to revisit the notion of justice because she made the mistake "To slay herself, that should have slain her foe" (1827).

"Suicide" does not emerge as a term until the seventeenth century. Instead, terms such as "self-murder" or "self-slaughter" were used, and the Latin "*felo de se*" (literally, "felon of oneself" because the act was a felony) was used often in legal and medical contexts. Although attitudes toward suicide were softening and the act was perceived increasingly as a secular concern, one can hear in these terms the sense of suicide as a crime. The bodies of those who had committed suicide were typically buried outside consecrated ground, frequently at a crossroads, in a highway, or along a boundary of some kind. The corpse was often desecrated with a stake driven through it.[42] One contemporary writes:

> to bury such as lay violent hands upon themselves, in or near to highways, with a stake thrust through their bodies, to terrify all passengers, by that so infamous and reproachful a burial, not to make their final passage out of this present world. The fear of not having burial, or having an ignominious and dishonourable burial, has ever frightened the bravest spirits in the world.[43]

The quotation alerts us to the parallel between the highway upon which the travelers will see the body of the suicide and the notion of a passage that individuals would take to the underworld. Once more, we see an example of how the afterlife is conceived in terms of the living world. The afterlife is again made sense of through the terms of the living world, and the dead are put into the service of instructing the living. At the same time, people here are "spirits" in this world. It reminds the reader of our status as living with death. The stake was also thought to pin the ghost to the body and make it unable to haunt nearby locations, though of course the existence of ghosts was debated during the period as Protestant discourses largely denied the existence of such phantoms. While many bodies of suicides were buried at crossroads, there was no clear-cut answer about what to do with the bodies and where these souls would go. As noted in the Introduction, Ophelia is buried in consecrated ground and thus assumed to rest there until Judgment Day, because a human tribunal judges it appropriate. In the case of Ophelia, playgoers might not be surprised to hear that her status can influence her place of burial.[44] The grave digger notes, "If this had not been a gentlewoman, she should have been buried out o' Christian burial" (5.1.23). The connection of one's class and wealth to one's status in the afterlife invokes the operations of indulgences, that medieval practice where payment to the church was thought to hurry deceased loved ones' passage through Purgatory. Ophelia, like Lucrece, presents a complex case study because her despair that led to suicide seems to be attributed to the distress caused by another person. From a Catholic theological point of view, one's earthly deeds and weight of required actions could have an effect on one's fate after death. Cardinal Wolsey, in *Henry VIII*, remarks that his duties are "a burden / Too heavy for a man that hopes for heaven" (3.2.385–6).

John Donne's defense of suicide *Biathanatos* (written 1607–1608, published 1647) names on the title page its "paradox or thesis, that self-homicide is not so naturally sin, that it may never be otherwise."[45] Donne's text "defends, under certain circumstances, the act of suicide as a legitimate Christian Practice."[46] Shakespeare's plays involve characters killing themselves in both Christian and non-Christian cultural contexts and often with moral ambiguity. We see in these instances how "performance offered a way to bring alternative forms of civil society to mind, to reimagine community and, as a consequence, to crystallize new powers of critical, embodied social thought into historical actuality."[47] In fact, placing many of these suicides in the context of previous or foreign cultures may have allowed for safer dialogue of polemic subjects.

Fantasies of the Afterlife in *Measure for Measure*

Measure for Measure represents what scholars term "a problem play," because it does not fit neatly into a single genre. During the course of the plot, good people have suffered, and the play ends on an ambiguous note. While it ends with a marriage proposal, we do not hear Isabella's response to the Duke and are left unsure whether she would prefer life in a domestic household instead of one in a convent. The larger plot of *Measure for Measure* intermingles elements of tragedy and comedy, and we find a similar collision of opposing elements in Claudio's meditation on his fate after death. Like many characters in the play, his storyline is characterized by suffering. His thoughts, in turn, articulate a series of collisions—between the living world and the afterlife, between sex and death, between the known and the unknown, and between reality and fantasy.

Before providing a lengthy description of what he believes to await him after death, Claudio states that "If I must die, / I will encounter darkness as a bride, / And hug it in mine arms" (3.1.81–3). The lines draw our attention to the links between sex and death that pervade early modern (and other) literature. For Claudio specifically, the vision of death as a loving bride has purchase on the circumstances that have resulted in his imprisonment and death sentence. On the most basic level, he and his lover Juliet have had sex which is perceived to be out of wedlock and now he must die. On a more complex level, he has impregnated Juliet; so his death matters less than if she were not pregnant, because his *self* will continue in the child. On yet another level, he imagines that the experience of death will resemble sex with a woman (though, as someone sentenced to die, he expects never to have sex again). While he ultimately pictures the afterlife as a traumatic environ alternatively fiery and frozen, Claudio initially links death to eroticism, echoing Cleopatra's suicide scene where the phrase "The stroke of death is a lover's pinch" points to the early modern commonplace of conflating sex and death (5.2.290). While the terms of the afterlife might be to some extent directed by one's theology, the profound unknowability of the afterlife offers degrees of freedom where Claudio and Cleopatra can imagine their transition as an erotic and potentially pleasurable experience.

Just as Hamlet describes the afterlife as unknown ("The undiscovered country from whose bourn / No traveller returns, puzzles the will, / And makes us rather bear those ills we have / Than fly to others that we know not of?"), Claudio at first describes the destination of souls as unknown: "Ay, but to die, and go we know not where" (3.1.81–4, 3.1.118).

However, he goes on to offer concrete descriptions of the possible fates of the body and the soul:

> To lie in cold obstruction, and to rot;
> This sensible warm motion to become
> A kneaded clod, and the dilated spirit
> To bathe in fiery floods, or to reside
> In thrilling region of thick-ribbèd ice;
> To be imprisoned in the viewless winds,
> And blown with restless violence round about
> The pendent world; or to be worse than worst
> Of those that lawless and incertain thought
> Imagine howling—'tis too horrible! (3.1.119–28)

Note that *Hamlet* and *Measure for Measure* make similar, paradoxical moves with regard to knowability of the afterlife. Hamlet claims that no one has ever returned from death, but the ghost of his father has just described to him in broad strokes a deeply unpleasant Purgatory. Claudio claims not to know where souls go, but then he describes the location in rich sensory detail. Claudio's depiction of the afterlife resembles a prison but trades the walls for an open space and perhaps translates his inner torment to an outer one. The afterlife—for Hamlet, for Claudio, and for other Shakespearean characters—might strike one as filled with contradiction and largely the stuff of personal fantasy. It represents a purely unknowable space, yet the space of death is used as a screen upon which to project the experience of living. As Michael Neill puts it, the speech in *Measure for Measure* offers "incarnations of formlessness itself, of the kind of death for which the imagination of a Claudio struggles to find metaphors."[48] Language is insufficient to depict the afterlife, yet the impulse remains to articulate it in some way.[49]

When the speech ends with "Imagine howling—'tis too horrible!," Claudio emphasizes that he does not know what comes after death and he does not want to know. Claudio seems to admit freely that the hellish afterlife he imagines is a fiction, and this admission echoes early modern debates about whether hell was a place of endless suffering. Christian writers began to doubt whether God's mercy would allow eternal torment, while others wondered if an eternity in hell was too close to the eternal life promised by heaven.[50] Ideas about the afterlife were diverse and increasingly fractured during Shakespeare's time. As Peter Marshall observes, during the seventeenth century, "an increasing number of English religious radicals would be prepared to reject the very notion of a localized afterlife, to assert that Heaven and Hell were no more than spiritual states experienced in this life."[51] As already noted, what Claudio depicts as occurring after death could very well describe his current state. His once "delighted spirit" that could engage in "sensible warm motion" certainly now finds itself "*imprisoned*."

The idea, then, that Claudio will welcome death as a bride is a puzzling one. This is especially true in the context of a dominant Renaissance religiosity that "has at its core the belief that love cannot transcend the mortal world" because couples would not reunite in the flesh after death.[52] Perhaps, if Claudio does not believe he will be reunited with his lover Juliet, he simply finds it reassuring to picture a lover welcoming him after death. However, the afterlife he pictures is a space of torment. Paul Morrison posits that *Measure for Measure* is the "most problematic of 'problem' plays," going on to argue that "what positively elevates it to the status of a perverse play—is its unabashed eroticization of artificially constructed and externally imposed strictures."[53] Life and death, as well as pleasure and pain, conflate in Claudio's prison-based fantasies of the afterlife. Montaigne asserts, "You are *in* death while you are *in* life," continuing "after life, you are dead, but during life, you are dying: and death touches the dying more harshly than the dead, in more lively a fashion and more essentially."[54] We hear echoes of this idea in *Romeo and Juliet*, when Capulet asserts that "Life, living, all is death's" (4.4.67). The notion also links to Donne's last sermon, where he describes how "we have a winding-sheet [burial shroud] in our mother's womb which grows with us from our conception, and we come into the world wound up in that winding-sheet, for we come to seek a grave." Montaigne also says, "To practise death is to practise freedom. A man who has learned how to die has unlearned how to be a slave."[55] Is it liberating for Claudio to dwell on death, to be "absolute for death" as the Duke urges him? Or does his imprisonment and contemplation of death simply bring into focus the similitude between life and death? There seems to be no escaping death or prison in this play, even in the marriages that mark the narrative resolution. As Sarah Beckwith puts it, "the marriages that conventionally end comedy are a punishment woven into the penitential investigations of the play, made necessary because sex is seen under the sign of sin."[56] In this play where Claudio fantasizes of death as his bride, coupling in this life and departing from this life ultimately conflate.

When Isabella visits Claudio in his cell, she tells him that he will suffer "perpetual durance" even if he is freed, explaining the weight he will have to bear in the knowledge that she would have slept with Angelo (3.1.66). "Durance," the *Oxford English Dictionary* informs us, denotes "forced confinement, imprisonment, constraint," and thus Isabella frames her brother's life after imprisonment as not very different from his current circumstances.[57] Shortly after this exchange, Claudio depicts life after death as "To be imprisoned in the viewless winds" (3.1.124). Thus, his current state and the two possible outcomes of his situation all share qualities of a state of torment. If Isabella sleeps with Angelo, Claudio will be sentenced to a type of psychic cell while she will be sentenced to a type of living hell. Indeed, Angelo is framed as a demonic paramour dealing out "devilish mercy" while enshrouded in "the cunning livery of hell" (3.1.63, 3.1.93). Karmen MacKendrick suggests that "death impends as an unimaginable event" and one that represents the ultimate discontinuity from those we love.[58] It is the threat of death—Claudio's execution or the living deaths that Isabella describes—that enable frank conversation between siblings. As Claudio and Isabella implore each other to consider the implications of the devil's bargain they face, we see an unpleasant testing of the expected loving bond between sister and brother. Yet MacKendrick reminds us, "[w]e can love only in the face of death" because "we can face the vertigo of death together."[59] For this brother and sister, the afterlife offers a conceptual space where they can project how their fates intertwine.

As we saw earlier in this book, suicide occupies an ambiguous position in Shakespeare's work. Suicide appears across the works not only as an act but also as a contemplated act. Isabella posits suicide as an alternative to giving her body up to Angelo this way:

> That is, were I under the terms of death,
> Th'impression of keen whips I'd wear as rubies,
> And strip myself to death as to a bed

> That longing have been sick for, ere I'd yield
> My body up to shame. (2.4.100–4)

It is an evocative passage that can be read in several ways. On the one hand, Isabella models the type of strict asceticism she could expect from convent life. Note, though, that her suffering has an erotic quality. Stripping herself to death links to Claudio's description of meeting death as a lover and resonates with George Bataille's notion that eroticism involves "assenting to life up to the point of death."[60] When Angelo tells her that her brother consequently must die, she replies:

> And 'twere the cheaper way.
> Better it were a brother died at once
> Than that a sister, by redeeming him,
> Should die for ever. (2.4.106–9)

These lines play with the multiple meanings of the word "die." Isabella indicates that to have sex with Angelo would mean for her to commit a sin and thus experience the death of her soul. Such an act would have implications for the afterlife as sex out of wedlock could guarantee punishment after death. The lines have an added level of complexity when we recognize "die" as early modern slang for an orgasm. Isabella implies that she might experience this from coupling with Angelo, but this pleasure is unwanted by her.

The Duke's visit to the imprisoned Claudio offers a crucial flash-point for mapping out the colliding energies and opposing elements that circulate throughout the play. As part of his case that Claudio should be "absolute for death," the Duke explains to Claudio that "Thou art not thyself, / For thou exist'st on many a thousand grains / That issue out of dust" (3.1.19–21). The counsel resonates with the logic of Genesis 3:19, which tells us, "for out of it wast thou taken, because thou art dust, and to dust shalt thou return."[61] To answer Hamlet's question, "what is this quintessence of dust?", one might say "ourselves" not just in a speculative sense (where we will return to dust upon death) but also to admit that dust is also a reflection of our current selves, an encounter with ourselves as dead (2.2.310). The material dust is, after all, comprised largely from dead tissue from our bodies and the bodies of other living things. As we age and discard skin or hair, we realize that our bodies are gradually dying and thus the moment of death simply punctuates a long process. The Duke's conversation with Claudio echoes Montaigne's assertion that the living are already deceased, and the invocation of dust underscores that the living world itself is comprised of the dead.[62]

The Duke concludes this long speech by remarking, "Yet in this life / Lie hid more thousand deaths: yet death we fear, / That makes these odds all even" (3.1.39–41). The lines articulate a similar idea found in those famous lines from *Julius Caesar*, "Cowards die many times before their deaths; / The valiant never taste of death but once" (2.2.32–3). Ernest Hemingway would later reflect upon the lines and have one of his characters state, "'The coward dies a thousand deaths, the brave but one' [The man who first said that] knew a great deal about cowards but nothing about the brave. The brave dies perhaps two thousand deaths if he's intelligent. He simply doesn't mention them."[63] In all three instances, acknowledging the constant presence of death is central to an individual's self-fashioning. Indeed, the Duke must discuss death in order to help Claudio understand the price of love and the claim that the legal system has on love. Claudio's union with his lover Juliet offered respite within the private sphere of the couple, but their coupling made them the object of the state. So, perhaps it makes sense that when Claudio imagines freedom from his cell, he generates his own fictions of the afterlife that involve a romantic union. Eric S. Mallin suggests that "Claudio has no discernible relationship with God," and this may explain why the otherworldly space of hell becomes the subject of his fantasies.[64]

The interpretation explored thus far builds upon but diverges from Jonathan Dollimore's reading of *Measure for Measure*. He suggests that the exchange between Claudio and the Duke dramatizes "an ideology of social control, converting transgressive desire into complete submission to authority, even to the point of welcoming death."[65] If Claudio here is a subject who concedes to the state's control over his life and death, the visit by the Duke/Friar does emphasize religion-as-institution's role in bolstering state power and religion-as-fiction's role in promising a release from the perils of the living world. By having a duke masquerading as a friar, using the afterlife as a tool to affect the actions of the living, the play dramatizes how the "process of reform in England created a body politic in which the ostensibly secular sphere, of monarchy and magistracies that were 'of the world', were closely entwined with the supernatural."[66] The Duke frames existence as a perpetual state of wanting, where "Happy thou art not, / For what thou hast not, still thou striv'st to get, / And what thou hast, forget'st" (3.1.21–4). Dollimore reads the Duke's lines to signal that "[d]eath is the eternal release from an identity and a desire—identity *as* desire—tormented by mutability and founded on the contradiction that life is a kind of death."[67] We can extend and complicate Dollimore's logic when we focus on the afterlife, "the life to come" as Macbeth puts it, as a state characterized by desire that mirrors the living world (1.7.7). Indeed, Claudio's position in the living world is co-constituted by his imagined position in the afterlife. His proximity to death, both in the sense that he may shortly face the executioner and in the sense that he contemplates death's welcome embrace, represents a physical and psychic orientation. We may read life and death as opposing forces, as Dollimore does, while also admitting their dynamic relationship as they generate fantasies that reveal how truly similar they are to each other.

When Isabella tells her brother that "Lord Angelo, having affairs in heaven, / Intends you for his swift ambassador," she points to the state's control over Claudio's time of death (3.1.54–5). She also takes up the metaphor from *Hamlet* of the afterlife as another country, suggesting that it represents a location to which Angelo may send Claudio but over which he maintains no control. Julia Reinhard Lupton has argued that Claudio's "secret consensual union" with Juliet is a form of association that has not only "elude[d] the direct supervision of the state and its church, but also occurred beyond the household."[68] We can extend Lupton's claim to describe also Claudio longing for an erotic union with death. To die in an embrace with a lover would better resemble a private affair of the heart than a public execution. Such a death would be an escape from state control, even to a limited extent. Such a fantasy is made possible because the afterlife (like the exact nature of erotic or romantic unions) is characterized by unknowability. Love is what Leo Bersani calls an "unaccountable, unclassifiable" object; so is the afterlife. For Bersani and for Freud, "There are degrees of self-shattering, ranging from such examples of sexually stimulating simulation [...] as intellectual strain, verbal disputes, and railway travel, to the ultimate devastation of the ego and the subject in death."[69] While the Freudian perspective places death and sexual stimulation along a spectrum of self-shattering activities, the two share the ability to transport us into an unknowable space, one that is not only self-shattering but also classification-shattering. Angelo urges Isabella to demonstrate her submission by "putting on the destined livery," a phrase which conflates sex and death because here the play suggests "the procreative sheets—and the swaddling clothes, and the burial shroud—are indeed the destined livery of each human being" (2.4.138).[70]

In these examples from *Measure for Measure*, the contemplation of death allows characters to articulate the contradictions and paradoxes that characterize the situations in which they find themselves. At the resolution of the play, the Duke's famous speech will announce, "'An Angelo for Claudio, death for death'. / Haste still pays haste, and leisure answers leisure; / Like doth quit like, and measure still for measure" (5.1.406–8). The line derives from Matthew 7:2, which states, "For with what judgment ye judge, ye shall be judged, and with what measure ye mete, it shall be measured unto you again." The biblical source matches like elements and speaks to issues of justice. The Duke's speech matches both like and unlike elements and speaks to the at-times competing elements that have driven the plot of the play. The larger notion of "measure for measure" invites us to draw equivalency between different actions, experiences, and ways of being. Tracing discussions of the death's approach in the play helps us see the afterlife as a site where unlike elements—including death, love, marriage, imprisonment, and freedom—collide and find new equivalencies. Fantasies about life after death, in turn, allow individuals to come to terms with the uncertainty that marks both the living world and the world beyond it.

2

At the Gateway to the Afterlife

Encounters with bodies of the dead spark consideration of the fate of the departed, both in terms of how they survive in living memory and of what their fate might be in the world beyond. The tomb especially represents an intriguing location in the geography of the afterlife. On one level, it offers to the dead an extension of life within the world of the living, in the sense that it perpetuates memory of the departed. On another level, it allows the living to feel as if they are still in the presence of the dead and perhaps understand themselves on the threshold of a world they will one day encounter. In the early modern period, tombs played a central role in the culture of mourning. In fact, many of Shakespeare's most memorable scenes take place in tombs.

Funeral monuments, including tombs, offer a flashpoint for differing attitudes toward the dead during the Reformation. Some Protestant Reformers thought that epitaphs and tombs were too extravagant. John Calvin, for example, sought to be buried in an unmarked grave. However, others saw funeral monuments as vital physical objects capable of transmitting moral instruction and articulating beliefs. Martin Luther suggested that cemeteries should function as places that should "inspire devotion in those who go there."[1] A royal statute in 1560 stated that the intention of church monuments should be "to show a memory to the posterity of the persons there buried."[2] The statute reiterates a concept of the funeral monument that reaches back to classical antiquity. The ancient Greek word for tomb is *sema*, which means a sign meant to communicate meaning. The term *soma*, which means "body," was also sometimes used in place of *sema*.[3] In the interchangeability of the two terms, we can hear how the tomb means to signify the body of the departed and how both the tomb and the body carry meaningful messages for the living. While some early moderns felt that the communication of such meanings might be done in too decorative a way, tombstones were largely exempt from the post-Reformation regulations that demanded simplicity in visual design, given that they were regarded as commemorative (rather than religious) in nature.[4]

Despite some concern about their extravagance, grave markers throughout the sixteenth- and seventeenth-centuries increasingly showcased details about the deceased's life as well as transmitted moral instruction for the living. Funeral monuments became more individualized, moving away from the use of generic imagery to featuring portraits or more personalized imagery meant to reflect the deceased's life or beliefs.[5] Epitaphs and shrines are themselves narratives about a person's life that are to some extent constructed, given that they represent how the person would like to be remembered or how others would like to remember her or him. The mid-sixteenth century witnessed a surge in antiquarianism, as a passion for preserving and documenting the past motivated writers on the subject to express specific concern that these commemorative, material art pieces were not being effectively preserved. For example, William Camden's *Brittania* (1586) and John Weever's *Ancient Funeral Monuments* (1631), which chronicled grave markers in England, lamented that London tomb makers were not effectively documenting their work and urged those who discovered epitaphs to write them down to preserve them. These engraved narratives of individual lives, then, were perceived as crucial elements in the larger story of England's history. Inventories of epitaphs have been collected since the seventeenth century, but many of the monuments that formed the contexts for the delivery and reception of these epitaphs have been lost.[6] In fact, Weever's book contains over 900 pages of descriptions of epitaphs and grave markers, many of which are no longer extant. It is this very decay of tombstones against which George Herbert's poem "Church Monuments" warns when it depicts grave markers joining the same "fellowship of dust" as the bodies they contain.[7]

Just as London was the hub for many new theatrical enterprises, a great deal of the early modern funeral monument production took place in the city, as its rapid growth in living population also meant rapid growth not only of playgoers, but also of the dead.[8] The presence of parish churchyards throughout London, historically hubs of communal activities including burial of the dead, established "close cohabitation of the living and the dead" in the early modern urban environment.[9] As Joseph Roach observes, Shakespeare is writing just before a "revolutionary spatial paradigm: the segregation of the dead from the living."[10] Because the emergence of "architectural spaces that effectively masked the dead (and later the dying) from the daily experience of the living" commenced during the eighteenth century in London, we can imagine that Shakespeare's audience had a more intimate sense of the nearness of death and of the omnipresence of the dead than would generations to follow. At least since classical antiquity and probably much earlier, tombs have offered a means to render—as Mario Erasmo evocatively puts it—"the dead as undead" because they foster "the ongoing social relationships between the living and the dead in which the living continue to perpetuate an identity for the deceased through memorials, epitaphs, and graveside rituals."[11] Indeed, tombs not only co-located dead individuals with living ones but also brought the bustle of the living world in close proximity with the tranquility of the afterlife. Funeral monuments not only functioned as communications from the dead to the living, but also offered opportunities to build community among the living. These edifices marked spaces where the living could gather to mourn and to reflect on their own place in history.

The spatial and temporal ambiguities of a tomb are nicely captured by Nicolas Poussin's painting "Les bergers d'Arcadie" ("The Shepherds in Arcadia") and other works reproducing the theme since the early modern period. Painted in 1637–1688, Poussin's image shows a group of shepherds gazing at a tomb whose epitaph reads, "*et in arcadia ego*" ("I am also in Arcadia").[12] There are different ways to interpret the inscription. We might take the "I" to be death, suggesting that the tomb is meant to remind us that death is everywhere, even in such lovely pastoral places as Arcadia. If we take the speaker to be the deceased, however, then the epitaph is reminding visitors that the dead person is *both* here in the grave and in the bliss of the afterlife. The group of shepherds around the tomb portrays how epitaphs not only spoke to groups of the living but also fostered dialogue among members of those groups who would visit sites where people were buried.

Early moderns had a strong sense of their own posterity, and many—possibly including Shakespeare himself—composed their own epitaphs before they died. The sixteenth century witnessed a boom in the production of gravestones as literacy rates increased and as post-Reformation funeral practices placed more emphasis on family and patrons memorializing the dead.[13] Indeed, the verb "to epitaph" and the noun "tombstone" both emerged into the English language in the sixteenth century. The word *epitaph* itself stresses the importance of understanding the engraved text in its spatial and material context. The word comes to us from ancient Greek, where *epi-* means "on," "about," "around," or "near" and *-taph* means "sepulcher" or "tomb." These etymologies remind us that the monument's message is intended to be received within sight of the tomb itself. Before the 1500s, it was very rare for individuals to have a say regarding how their monument would be created. By the last half of the sixteenth century, it was commonplace for individuals to design or even construct their own monuments.[14] Shakespeare is buried in Holy Trinity Church in Stratford-Upon-Avon. His epitaph reads as a warning to those who visit:

> Good friend for Jesus sake forbear,
> To dig the dust enclosed here.
> Blessed be the man that spares these stones,
> And cursed be he that moves my bones.

Note here that the epitaph warns interlopers against moving the bones. In Shakespeare's time, it was common practice to move remains to make room for new dead. Especially given the early modern belief that the soul sleeps within the body, such an act calls into question the notion of resting in peace. There is also a monument to Shakespeare in the church, erected a few years after his death in 1621. It reads:

> Stay, passenger, why goest thou by so fast?
> Read, if thou can, whom envious death has placed
> Within this monument: Shakespeare, with whom
> Quick nature died, whose name does deck his tomb
> Far more than cost since all that he had written
> Leaves living art but page to serve his wit.

The inscription arrests the visitor with its opening line in English, which resonates with the *carpe diem* trope. Members of generations after Shakespeare find the fleeting nature of their lives thrown into relief both by the unaging stone monument to Shakespeare and by the paean to his "living page." The statue will inspire passers-by to remember and to read the author's work, which in turn perpetuates him in cultural and personal memory. In Chapter 5, we will return to this notion.

Giving Up the Ghost

The presence of a dying body allows characters to imagine the spirit passing from this life to the next. The dying individual is briefly in two places at once, dwelling in the body and out of the body. At the moment of death, we see characters "give up the ghost," to use a phrase that we hear in *King Henry VI Part III*. In that play, Richard reports how during a battle, a "noble gentleman gave up the ghost" (2.3.22). The phrase can be applied to an individual or a group. In *Julius Caesar*, we hear that "Their shadows seem / A canopy most fatal, under which/Our army lies ready to give the ghost" (5.1.86–8). The lines leave it intriguingly ambiguous whether the army is about to surrender or about to perish. "Give up the ghost" (or "give the ghost" in the second example here) is such an intriguing phrase because it implies surrender. To stay alive is a battle, and in fact the examples here both occur in martial contexts. "Give up" connotes yielding and also a sense of relief. The *Oxford English Dictionary* informs us that, since the twelfth century, the phrase "give up" has meant "to resign, surrender; to hand over, part with." Because the phrase insists that there is an essence inside of us that can migrate to new ways of being, "give up the ghost" implies the immortality of the soul. It also implies that we already contain ghosts. The phrase thus asserts not only that some part of us will always survive but also that some part of us is already dead, already constituted for its future residence in the afterlife. "Give up the ghost" is much older than Shakespeare. The phrase appears in "The Prioress's Tale" in Chaucer's *The Canterbury Tales*, and it can be found in the Bible too. In the Geneva Bible, Acts 12:23 describes how a man "was eaten of worms, and gave up the ghost."[15]

As the line from Acts makes clear, the notion of the soul as immortal stands in contrast to the visible decay of the body. Devoid of its "ghost" or life-giving spirit, the corpse evinces the power of *tempus edax rerum*, or time as the devourer of all things. This is the same power that drives the urgency of some of Shakespeare's sonnets, which caution the addressee against the dangers of time's "[d]evouring" capacities and warn that "nothing 'gainst time's scythe can make defense" (19.1, 12.13). In *Measure for Measure*, Claudio's depiction of himself dying only "To lie in cold obstruction, and to rot" reminds us that the body is the medium through which many of Shakespeare's characters try to make sense of impending death. Indeed, the fate of dead bodies is an issue that concerns many characters, including the king in *Richard II*, who laments:

> Let's talk of graves, of worms and epitaphs,
> Make dust our paper, and with rainy eyes
> Write sorrow on the bosom of the earth.
> Let's choose executors and talk of wills—
> And yet not so, for what can we bequeath
> Save our deposèd bodies to the ground? (3.2.141–6)

In this speech, mortality invites contemplation about how one's legacy or intentions can be carried forward through funeral monuments and written wills. At the same time, the speech emphasizes the futility of such efforts for the dead. Worms consume bodies. Paper decays. Tears are temporary. The earth absorbs the soul's physical vessel. The body is thus a marker for prospective loss, as individuals speculate how the world will progress without their living frame, and retrospective loss, as individuals treat the corpse as an object of mourning. When we encounter a reference to a dead body in Shakespeare's work, we should take it as invitation to explore the dialectical collision of opposing energies. As Susan Zimmerman argues, the corpse renders visible and then problematizes the "slippery distinctions that seem to originate in bodily phenomena: outer and inner, visible and invisible, tangible and intangible, substantial and insubstantial, continuous and discontinuous."[16] The dead body can inspire maudlin reflection, as it does for Richard II, and it can also serve perverse intentions. Take, for example, the troubling scene in *Richard III* where the protagonist woos Anne in the presence of the corpse of Henry VI. The body creates an opportunity for him to feign contrition in order to transmute her hatred into love, as well as to emphasize that marrying her husband's murderer may be her best strategy for avoiding a similar fate. The corpse signifies the past, in the sense that it shows how ruthless Richard can be, and it signifies the future in the sense that she may need to ally herself with someone if she will survive in the new court environment.

The dead body can thus be charged with multiple valences, as we see in a touching but also comedic scene in *Henry V* when Hostess Quickly describes the death of Sir John Falstaff. Although the ghost or soul cannot be seen as it exits the body, characters such as her imagine this occurrence as life leaves the body. It is at once basic anatomy and also a salacious description for such a voracious figure. He first appears to be descending into a second childhood:

> I saw him fumble with the sheets, and play with flowers, and smile upon his fingers' end, I knew there was but one way. For his nose was as sharp as a pen, and a babbled of green fields. (2.3.13–17)

This man-child resembles the archetype from Jaques' "Seven Ages of Man" speech, where the old man enters a second childhood as he approaches death:

> Last scene of all,
> That ends this strange, eventful history,
> Is second childishness and mere oblivion,
> Sans teeth, sans eyes, sans taste, sans everything. (2.7.163–6)

The description of "oblivion" and the physical body "sans everything" in terms of awareness parallels the experience of physical death and speaks to the experience of Falstaff's demise. After exhibiting his state of delusion, the old man then cries out: "'God, God, God' three or four times" (2.3.18–19). The Hostess then reports how she touched the dying man's legs,

> I put my hand into the bed and felt them, and they were as cold as any stone.
> Then I felt to his knees, and so up'ard and up'ard, and all was as cold as any stone. (2.3.22–5)

She goes into a detailed description of the old man's body giving up the ghost. We have an erotic pun operating here, as "stone" functioned as slang for testicles. This old, bawdy man has the joy of being felt-up one last time as he dies, and his crying out resembles that of an orgasm. One can imagine how this whole description might be performed in a light-hearted or melancholy way. We can read the scene as a meditation about how the living person transmutes into an object upon death. In a flow that we will see reversed in the resurrection scene in *The Winter's Tale*, this once lively man turns to stone.

Following Friends and Loved Ones into the Afterlife

In *Henry V*, the death of Sir John Falstaff spurs a conversation among the living about what happens after death as well as an expressed hope that individuals can reunite in the afterlife. Upon the death of his tavern companion, Bardolph declares, "Would I were with him, wheresome'er he is, / either in heaven or in hell" (2.3.7–8). The death of another has one long for reunion. First, though, this group must determine where the soul of their friend has gone.

The Hostess responds to Bardolph's question with an answer that sounds partially like logical reasoning and partially like pure fantasy. She suggests,

> Nay, sure, he's not in hell. He's in Arthur's bosom, if ever man went to Arthur's bosom. A made a finer end, and went away an it had been any christom child. (2.3.9–12)

A way of reassuring each other about the death of their friend is to insist that he has gone to heaven. The Hostess seems to mis-speak when she says "Arthur's bosom" rather than "Abraham's bosom," a destination for good Christians where they rested until the Resurrection. Luke 16:22 reads, "So it was that the beggar died, and was carried by the angels to Abraham's bosom."[17] But her malapropism suggests that she may also be thinking of "King Arthur," as Falstaff was a knight. Invoking Arthur gives her statement the characteristics of a eulogy, a speech of praise at someone's funeral, because to be embraced by the legendary king implies a knightly reputation for the bungling drunk. It also suggests an alternative afterlife for knights. Her choice of "Arthur" introduces another interesting ambiguity here. The mythical Arthur is supposedly not dead but actually healing in the fairy otherworld Avalon, from where he is supposed to return in England's time of need. To place Falstaff in Avalon, not in the Christian heaven, is yet another indication of multiple afterlives and also could constitute a wish for resurrection. To be placed in Avalon with Arthur would not only mean that Falstaff now dwells in the idealized realm of medieval knights but also that he might one day return. Whatever the case, the death of the friend unites the tavern friends in mourning as they articulate shared desires and values. As Philippe Ariès puts it, "death is not a purely individual act, any more than life is. Like every great milestone in life, death is celebrated by a ceremony that is always more or less solemn and whose purpose is to express the individual's solidarity with his family and community."[18] Falstaff's death is witnessed by one friend and then testified about to others who were aware of his imminent passing. While there may yet be a formal funeral for the jovial knight, it seems a fitting ceremony that his friends should wish him well in front of the London tavern where he spent his days.

Bardolph wishes that he could follow his friend into the afterlife, and we can see this sentiment expressed in early modern public culture. For example, we find joint tombs for spouses and for friends throughout England. Headstones and engravings show their bodies side by side, sometimes sleeping, holding hands, or praying together.[19] Published after Shakespeare's death, John Dunton's *An Essay Proving We Shall Know Our Friends in Heaven* (1698) argues that heaven's state as a place of complete bliss can only be possible if we reunite with loved ones because "I am sure thy happiness cannot be complete 'til thy other half were also transported to heaven."[20] While Dunton refers to a spouse here, this same notion of *other half* or *other self* was frequently applied both to spouses and to friends in Shakespeare's time. Scripture is interestingly ambiguous about whether or not people would reunite in heaven. On the one hand, Matthew 22:30 states, "For in the resurrection they neither marry wives, nor wives are bestowed in marriage, but are as the Angels of God in heaven." A note clarifies that humans "shall be without bodies" in heaven and thus "neither marry nor be married." If there is no marriage in heaven and if humans do not have bodies, it seems unlikely that individuals would recognize each other or that there would be need for coupling. On the other hand, a note to 1 Corinthians 13:13 in the Geneva Bible explains that "in the life to come [...] there at length shall we truly and perfectly love both God, and one another."

Bardolph's and Dunton's hopes that loved ones reunite after death finds moving dramatization in *Henry V*. In response to Henry's request for news of the battle, Exeter reports on the death of two comrades-in-arms:

Suffolk first died, and York, all haggled over,
Comes to him, where in gore he lay insteeped,
And takes him by the beard, kisses the gashes
That bloodily did yawn upon his face,
And cries aloud, "Tarry, dear cousin Suffolk.
My soul shall thine keep company to heaven.
Tarry, sweet soul, for mine, then fly abreast,
As in this glorious and well-foughten field
We kept together in our chivalry". (4.6.11–19)

The affection we see here between two friends of the same sex would not strike early moderns as strange.[21] Such closeness, especially among knights such as these, dates back to the medieval period. For example, *The Westminster Chronicle* describes the 1391 deaths of William Neville and John Clanvowe.[22] Neville is described as dying of "inconsolable sorrow" in Constantinople two days after the passing of his friend and fellow knight Clanvowe, "whom he loved no less than himself."[23] The reciprocity between the two noblemen is emblematized by Neville's insistence on dying in the same village where Clanvowe died and the two would eventually occupy a joint tomb adorned with an engraved image of the two men facing as if about to kiss and with their two shields overlapping. The *Chronicle*'s description of Neville refusing to take food after the death of his friend symbolizes that he shows no interest in nourishment at all in a world without Clanvowe.

So, too, does Shakespeare's knight die to join his friend (Figure 2.1). In a gesture that intermingles loving embrace and a welcome of death,

So did he turn, and over Suffolk's neck
He threw his wounded arm, and kissed his lips,
And so espoused to death, with blood he sealed
A testament of noble-ending love. (4.6.24–7)

The extent to which the scene moved Exeter is evidenced when he reflects, "And all my mother came into mine eyes / And gave me up to tears" (4.6.31–2). David L. Eng and David Kazanjian remark that "loss is inseparable from what remains, for what is lost is known only by what remains of it, by how these remains are produced, read, and sustained."[24] The "remains" of these two men are *reproduced*, *read*, and

Figure 2.1. "Henry V (IV, 6, the Duke of York mourns the death of Suffolk)," Alexandre Bida (nineteenth century).

Courtesy of the Folger Shakespeare Library.

sustained in the re-telling of the story of their deaths to the king and in their revivification in repeated performances of the play.

Given the danger faced by soldiers such as Suffolk and York, it is easy to see how war represents a particular time when humans find themselves especially close to death and thereby likely to contemplate the afterlife. Above, we saw the martial contexts in which variations of the phrase "give up the ghost" are used in Shakespeare. In other plays, the context of war inspires soldiers to imagine an afterlife and to wish for that world to be a site of reunion. In *Henry VI, Part III*, for example, Warwick and Oxford make a plan to meet in heaven. In *Henry VI, Part I*, too, John Talbot and his father commit to die together in battle and enter the afterlife jointly. The father exclaims, "Come, side by side together live and die, / And soul with soul from France to heaven fly." The way that "side by side" and "soul with soul" suggest the union of the family members tracks to the other pair of nouns in the sentence (4.5.54–5). "Live and die" are opposites, but the father and son hope that their joined status in life will guarantee the same in heaven.

Tombs, Statues, and Farewells in *Romeo and Juliet*

Upon the death of the two lovers at the end of the play, Romeo's father promises to "raise [Juliet's] statue in pure gold" (5.3.298) while Juliet's father reciprocates the promise, "As rich shall Romeo's by his lady's lie" (5.3.302). Such graven golden memorial images might seem like an affront to staunch Protestant beliefs that held against both funeral monuments and epitaphs. However, the funeral statues in *Romeo and Juliet* realize two fantasies: that the lovers have somehow survived in the earthly world and that they might be reunited after death.

Early on, the play signals that these lovers hover precariously close to the afterlife. For example, the Friar sees Juliet approach and describes her as someone who "[w]ill ne'er wear out the everlasting flint" (2.5.17). The sight of this young woman makes him think immediately of her death, as "flint" can refer to her funeral monument. While the decision to erect statues for the young lovers seems to come spontaneously to the minds of the fathers at the end of the play, she has already inspired Friar Laurence to think of her as a monument. We will return to these statues, and the tomb in which the final scene takes place, next. For now, though, let us notice how the afterlife haunts the play. The nearness of death for all the characters is underscored when Juliet greets the Friar with "Good even to my ghostly confessor" (2.5.21). He seems already dead, as she did to him.

This play is more than simply a story where two lovers die at the end. Rather, it interlaces love and death from the very start, tapping into an existing early modern interest in the overlap between these two forces. Consider for a moment the tradition in Renaissance art known as "death and the maiden." A popular trope in visual imagery depicted evocative encounters between a skeleton (signifying death) and a barely dressed or entirely naked woman. Such images remind viewers of the closeness between death and eroticism, an overlap dwelt upon in many literary texts within the early modern canon. Think about, for example, how Cyril Tourneur's *The Atheist's Tragedy* (1611) features two lovers who meet in a charnel house and use death's heads as pillows when they sleep. In that play, the tomb represents a place to think on death but also to stir what Freud would see as the opposite of the death drive: erotic desire. We find this dynamic in *Romeo and Juliet*, as well, where one of its most romantic scenes occurs in a tomb at the end of the play.

Just as the Friar imagines Juliet as already situated in the afterlife, she contemplates Romeo's afterlife throughout the play. When Romeo says that he looks forward to their "sweet discourses in our times to come," Juliet responds "Methinks I see, now thou art so low / As one dead in the bottom of a tomb" (3.5.53–6). More than just seeing the living man as already dead, she envisions their future relations as taking place after his death. Juliet hopes for apotheosis for her lover when he dies, as he might achieve stellification and be transformed into a constellation of stars:

> Come, gentle night; come, loving, black-brow'd night,
> Give me my Romeo, and when I shall die,
> Take him and cut him out in little stars,
> And he will make the face of heaven so fine
> That all the world will be in love with night
> And pay no worship to the garish sun. (3.2.20–5)

Metamorphosis into stars or other heavenly substance was a common resolution for dying figures in the myths of classical antiquity. For example, Orion, Castor, and Pollux all achieve immortality when transformed by the gods into stars. In turn, stellification became a frequent trope within the literature of praise in the early modern period.[25] Like the Friar's vision of a dead Juliet, this vision of Romeo presages his status as a statue at the end of the play. She desires that he become the object of display for a living world that must appreciate his beauty. Julia Kristeva describes this story of the young lovers as one where "they spend less time loving each other than getting ready to die."[26] In *Romeo and Juliet*, death underscores the meaning of parting. Romeo boasts, "Then love-devouring death do what he dare – / It is enough I may but call her mine" (2.5.7–8). The threat of death creates urgency for erotic and romantic connection. Denis De Rougemont's reading of *Tristan and Iseult*, "unawares and in spite of themselves, the lovers have never had but one desire, the desire for death!," befits many critics' readings of *Romeo and Juliet.*[27]

When we reach the final scene of the play in the Capulet tomb, it is no surprise that the interactions are filled with romantic energies. Romeo's final line, "Thus with a kiss I die", echoes language we have already heard in *Othello* and *Venus and Adonis* (5.3.120). When the young lover encounters the seemingly dead Juliet, he dwells on the appearance of her body not only to assess her medical condition but also to lament the loss of their love relation:

> Death, that hath sucked the honey of thy breath,
> Hath had no power yet upon thy beauty.
> Thou art not conquered. Beauty's ensign yet
> Is crimson in thy lips and in thy cheeks,
> And death's pale flag is not advancèd there. (5.3.92–6)

In this body that he perceives to be dead, Romeo finds the echoes of his erotic desire still present. Francesco Robortello remarks, "there is an element of pleasure even in mourning and lamentation for the dead."[28] The extended martial metaphor embedded in "conquered" also emphasizes that desire is heightened by the inevitability of loss in that battle. Juliet looks enticing in her lifeless repose (a phenomenon that we will see again in the case of Cleopatra). Shakespeare's play was not necessarily unusual in this depiction. On Tuesday February 23, 1668/69, the diarist Samuel Pepys kisses the lips of the decayed body of the wife of Henry V, Queen Katherine of Valois, who died in 1457. The fact that her soul has departed does not deter him from being titillated as he finds himself afterward "reflecting upon it that I did kiss a Queen, and that this was my birth-day, thirty-six years old, that I did first kiss a Queen."[29] His birthday seems a fit time to celebrate his life in contrast to the commemoration of someone else's deathday. The themes find expression on the stage as well. In *The Second Maiden's Tragedy* (1611), a character simply called Tyrant removes the corpse of a character named Lady from a tomb with the intent to have sex with her. Govianus, the good king in the story kills Tyrant. While the story's strange elements of necrophilia may sound extreme, we can see its mix of elements—the site of the tomb as one that intermingles sexual desire and contemplations of death—to be not altogether alien to an early modern diarist such as Samuel Pepys or an early modern audience familiar with *Romeo and Juliet.*

Romeo's sense that Juliet's dead body still indicates desirousness implies that their love for each other can transcend death and thereby foreshadows the parents' decision to immortalize the lovers as funereal statues. Dollimore remarks that "this play is not just about desire between two people, but about desire itself as a fantasy-projection, a wish-fulfilment complete with perverse implications."[30] For these young lovers, to fully realize their attraction for each other is to join each other in death. Kristeva frames *Romeo and Juliet* as a text where "[d]eath, like a final orgasm, like a full night, waits at the end of the play."[31] So, in some ways, funerary statues best represent the nature of the lovers' desire. The play's conclusion and especially its funereal statues are foreshadowed throughout the early scenes in the play, even in their first kiss. Romeo describes his lips as "two blushing pilgrims," and Juliet responds with discussion of "saints" and "holy palmers" (1.5.94, 97–8). Thus, the lovers couple in a context immediately rich in the language of Catholic worship, idolatry, and religious materialism. However, the deathly monuments to Romeo and Juliet surprisingly uncouple these lovers in the afterlife.

The statues that the parents plan to erect, while seemingly serving as a testimony to the couples' love, render the couple visibly separated and, further, do not show them at rest. As noted earlier, joint tombs for friends and lovers commonly show them touching or asleep together. Ramie Targoff argues that "not only are the lovers denied any hint of a transcendent afterlife, but they are also denied the intimacy of a private tomb."[32] In a period when the certainty of lovers reuniting after death was called into question, the play cryptically positions their rush toward the afterlife as resulting in eternal separation. If the concept of "*et in arcadia ego*" encourages us to imagine the dead as simultaneously in their tomb and in a world beyond the living, the imagery here suggests that the only true connection for Romeo and Juliet was at their time of death.

The Anti-Memorial in *Timon of Athens*

Timon of Athens offers a striking depiction of the tomb and its relationship to communal memory. Unlike most other characters in Shakespeare, Timon dies alone. He has no lover or friend rushing to join him, and no one but the audience is present as he perishes in the space where he lived as a hermit. It is true that in the ancient Greek world, including Athens, the dead typically were buried outside of the city, but Timon takes this alienation to the extreme.[33] He also takes control of how he will be encountered after death as he, like many early moderns, writes his own epitaph. Yet his self-made tomb strangely functions as what we might term an *anti-memorial*. His epitaph orders those who see it to both remember him and yet "seek not my name" (5.5.73).

A soldier who comes across Timon's burial place describes it to his general, Alcibiades, this way:

> My noble general, Timon is dead,
> Entomb'd upon the very hem o'th' sea;
> And on his grave-stone this insculpture, which
> With wax I brought away, whose soft impression
> Interprets for my poor ignorance. (5.5.66–70)

The "soft impression" here refers both to the copy of the epitaph and to the emotional effect that it has on the soldier. In its softness, it is both moving and also light, perhaps forgettable. Alcibiades reads the wax impression:

> Here lies a wretched corpse,
>   Of wretchd soul bereft.
> Seek not my name. A plague consume
>   You wicked catiffs left!

Here lie I, Timon, who alive
  All living men did hate.
Pass by and curse thy fill, but pass
  And stay not here thy gait. (5.5.71–8)

Timon despises all men, his epitaph tells us. Even in death, he repeats the announcement he made when he became a hermit: "I am *Misanthropos*, and hate mankind" (4.3.52). However, his epitaph nonetheless contains a lesson of moral instruction for the proud general who reads it. This message from the grave of a man who rejected friendly relations with others moves Alcibiades to seek peace with his enemies. Timon is a figure who should be remembered in posterity, not as a paragon to mimic but rather as a cautionary tale. Alcibiades initiates his march to reconciliation with an apostrophe to the deceased misanthrope:

On thy low grave, on faults forgiven. Dead
Is noble Timon, of whose memory
Hereafter more.
Bring me into your city,
And I will use the olive with my sword,
Make war breed peace, make peace stint war, make each
Prescribe to other as each other's leech.
Let our drums strike. (5.5.83–90)

Timon claims to not need a tomb, yet his burial place serves the function that Luther advocated for the graveyard: it should speak to those that visit it. We see such a notion also in *The Duchess of Malfi* (1612–1613), a play by Shakespeare's contemporary John Webster. A mysterious echo resounds from the Duchess' tomb in 5.3. Upon hearing this voice from the chamber of the dead woman, her widower, Antonio, disregards it. He says, "Echo, I will not talk with thee, / For thou art a dead thing"; the echo from the tomb replies, "Thou are a dead thing."[34] While Timon may insist that others forget him and while Antonio may try to ignore a voice from the place of the dead, both plays stress the impossibility of such refusals. In *The Duchess of Malfi*, the voice from the ignored tomb constitutes a premonition of Antonio's impending murder. In *Timon of Athens* (as in many texts, including Webster's) the words of the dead instantiate signs of the grave's function as *memento mori.*

The Tomb as Harbinger of the Future in *Titus Andronicus*

The action of one of Shakespeare's earliest plays, *Titus Andronicus* begins in a tomb and this sets the stage for the events that follow. Titus, a Roman military leader returning from war against the Goths, has come to bury his sons in the family tomb. Addressing himself, he emphasizes the duty of the living to the dead:

> Titus unkind, and careless of thine own,
> Why suffer'st thou thy sons, unburied yet
> To hover on the dreadful shore of Styx?
> Make way to lay them by their brethren.
> *They open the tomb.*
> There greet in silence, as the dead are wont,
> And sleep in peace, slain in your country's wars.
> O sacred receptacle of my joys,
> Sweet cell of virtue and nobility,
> How many sons hast thou of mine in store
> That thou wilt never render to me more! (1.1.86–95)

The "peace" described here might recall for us the sense of surrender inherent in the phrase "give up the ghost." Just as the dead sons hover on the shore of the river Styx waiting to have their memories erased as they cross over into the classical realm of the dead, the living are poised here to begin the process of putting the war behind them. Yet, here in this tomb, Titus counts his "store" of deceased and turns his attention to retribution. He condemns to death the eldest son of the Queen of the Goths, as recompense for the Roman dead.

At this point, we might pause at the notion of a play opening in a tomb. The setting might seem a better one for the end of a play, as we saw in *Romeo and Juliet* or even in *Timon of Athens*. Such a setting would be familiar as a place for endings among the plays of Shakespeare's contemporaries, too. For example, John Ford's *Love's Sacrifice* (1633) closes with the characters entering a tomb and the duke requesting, "set ope the tomb, that I may take / My last farewell, and bury griefs."[35] The tomb is a place for the end of narratives but also a crucial site toward which mourning energies can be directed and eventually released. In *Titus Andronicus*, we too see the tomb as a place of grief and hopes of resolution or closure on negative emotions. Yet this tomb, rather than being a place of resolution and burying of differences (as well as soldiers), figures as the starting point for the violence of the play. Indeed, the tomb is a place that initiates the cycle of death and retribution that drives the play to its terrible end.

In many ways, the tomb is an apt space to begin a revenge tragedy, as it is both a place where the bodies of many of the characters will ultimately be deposited and it also underscores how the economics of payback that undergirds revenge is a losing proposition. The Roman leader Lucius demands,

> Give us the proudest prisoner of the Goths,
> That we may hew his limbs and on a pile
> *Ad manes fratrum* sacrifice his flesh,
> Before this earthy prison of their bones,
> That so the shadows be not unappeased,
> Nor we disturbed with prodigies on earth. (1.1.96–101)

The dead make demands upon the living. Killing the son will bring peace to those that are dead and will interrupt lines of succession as no more children will be born from the sacrificed man. However, the logic ignores the fact that one of the results, or "prodigies," of this act will be the desire for revenge on the part of the sacrificed man's mother. Titus explains this to Tamora, the man's mother and Queen of the Goths, about the dead Romans: "Religiously they ask a sacrifice. / To this your son is marked, and die he must / T'appease their groaning shadows that are gone" (1.11.124–6). For the dead Romans ("groaning shadows") to move on to a space of forgetting and for the living Romans to move on from their losses, there must be more loss on the side of the Goths.

The solace of the dead and the living relies on a strange calculus that demands an excess of mourning. Titus' brother Marcus describes "this funeral pomp / That hath aspired to Solon's happiness," alluding to an Athenian statesman who supposedly said, "Call no man happy until he is dead" (1.1.176–7). One way to interpret Solon's statement is that we cannot judge someone's life except in retrospect once it is over. Another interpretation is that the dead are finally free of the suffering of life, and this seems to be the main thrust of Titus Andronicus' farewell to his dead sons:

> In peace and honour rest you here, my sons;
> Rome's readiest champions, repose you here in rest,

> Secure from worldly chances and mishaps.
> Here lurks no treason, here no envy swells,
> Here grow no damnèd drugs; here are no storms,
> No noise, but silence and eternal sleep.
> In peace and honour rest you here, my sons. (1.1.150–6)

He simultaneously describes a "here" that refers to the space of the silent tomb and to the afterlife. The term "here" counterintuitively indicates more than one space. That is, like the tomb that reads "*et in arcadia ego*," this speech acknowledges two simultaneous locations for the departed and implies that the tomb might be some early indication of how the afterlife might feel. However, Solon's phrase and Titus' speech point to darker meanings. Andrew Stark suggests that we understand Solon's point to claim "No matter how good your life has been, if it ended badly, that's what counts."[36] That is, all that matters is whether your story has a happy ending.

Stark's interpretation of Solon's aphorism applies well to *Titus Andronicus* and to the larger genre of revenge tragedy. In a narrative form where characters constantly attempt to attain *retributive justice*—that primitive form of ethical balancing based on *payback*—things must necessarily end badly. This rings true of Shakespeare's revenge tragedies and of the classical examples from which they take inspiration. Consider, for example, Aeschylus' *Oresteia*. The trilogy ends after a series of murders where one character kills the other in a chain of retributive violence. Driven by the ghost of Clytemnestra, furies torment Orestes until Athena orchestrates a court trial to end the succession of revenge killings. Renaissance playgoers familiar with the ancient play and the revenge tragedies that followed it would recognize the naiveté of Titus' speech. The General uses the suffering of souls in the afterlife as justification for continued violence in the world of the living. When it becomes a space of compounded deaths, the tomb is anything but a site of restfulness. It cannot end conflict when it demands further death or initiates a narrative. Acknowledging how Titus' desire for balance only demands imbalance helps us resolve what Colin Burrow identifies as "the strangely disarticulated relationship between Act I and the rest of *Titus Andronicus*."[37] The tomb and the imagined demands of the dead only fuel renewed demands among the living.

Fantasies of Deathly Reunion in *Antony and Cleopatra*

In the Turkish theater company Oyun Atölyesi's 2012 production of *Antony and Cleopatra* directed by Kemal Aydoğan at The Globe Theatre in London, Antony (played by Haluk Bilginer) surprisingly returns in ghostly form during Cleopatra's death scene. The choice in this production is highly evocative, suggesting on some level that the Egyptian's thrall is so strong that it could compel Antony to cross the barrier that separates our world from that of the dead. On another level, perhaps we somehow *need* this ghost in the final scene because Cleopatra continually addresses Antony—promising an impending reunion—during her death throes. As Roland Barthes remarks, "There is always, in the discourse upon love, a person whom one addresses, though this person may have shifted to the condition of a phantom or a creature still to come."[38]

In the case of this spectral Antony who appears on stage, he is both. He is a remnant of the past, an echo of possibilities now foreclosed. He is also the promise of an Antony yet-to-be, a central figure in both the lovers' fantasies that they will be reunited after death. Indeed, the play's title characters reconcile themselves to death by pre-emptively scripting their private experiences of a shared afterlife with each other. As we will see, such an impulse toward rebirth subtended by romantic coupling charges their death scenes with particularly erotic characteristics. Cleopatra especially translates her desire for death into a re-imagination of death itself as a pure form of desire.

It is striking the way that Cleopatra attempts to control not only the terms of her own demise but also how that demise will be remembered. Toward the end of the play, when in her tomb—a tomb that, of course, she has built for herself—she commands her servant to go and tell Antony that she has already died: "go tell him I have slain myself. / Say that the last I spoke was 'Antony'" (4.14.8–9). Ultimately, she will not actually speak his name as her last word, but we see here her desire not only for Antony to experience her passing as deeply personal but also—when she asks the servant to "bring me how he takes my death" (4.14.10)—to have the satisfaction of knowing how he will react to her demise. Given that Antony will in fact attempt suicide upon hearing the news, this play remixes the elements of *Romeo and Juliet*, where one lover will commit suicide upon false impression of the other's death. Here, though, rather than a tragic scene of misunderstanding, we have a scene of melodrama. We see the type of narcissism belonging to individuals who might long to attend their own funeral for the pleasure of seeing others mourn.

When the messenger relays to him the false news, Antony announces to his attendant, "Unarm, Eros. The long day's task is done, / And we must sleep" (4.15.35–6). While the attendant's name is actually Eros, we can understand Antony simultaneously to address love-in-the-abstract here. Indeed, when the Roman stabs himself—like Cleopatra later taking the asp to her breast—he dramatizes the situation where—as Jan Frans van Dijkhuizen has shown—pain and suffering can be linked "with the compelling nature of bodily sensations, with the ability of physical experiences to lend authority to otherwise abstract concepts."[39] Antony and Cleopatra need the sword and the asp to make material their heartbreak and to close their narratives at the climax, as it were. As he invites Eros to join him in suicide, Antony exclaims, "Eros!—I come, my queen:—Eros!" blurring our sense of whether we are witnessing sexual release or suicide (4.15.50). Cleopatra, too, will use this pun on "come"—as arrival and as sexual release—at the height of her own death scene, when she announces, "Husband, I come."

As he prepares to stab himself, Antony imagines a reunion with Cleopatra, calling out to her to

> [. . .] Stay for me.
> Where souls do couch on flowers we'll hand in hand,
> And with our sprightly port make the ghosts gaze.
> Dido and her Aeneas shall want troops,
> And all the haunt be ours. Come, Eros, Eros! (4.15.50–4)

He fantasizes that his and Cleopatra's passion will render them more lively than the other, jealous ghosts in the afterlife as these others follow them and ignore a nearby famous couple. As Stanley Wells notes, the afterlife as a place where "souls do couch on flowers" has us "picturing heaven as a place rather like the barge in which [Antony] had first seen [Cleopatra]."[40] Thus the Roman's fantasy of what happens after death to some extent dramatizes a moment unmarred by memory and still full of possibility. It does make a kind of sense, especially given Arthur Schopenhauer's notion that "every parting gives a foretaste of death, every coming together again a foretaste of the resurrection".[41] On one level, this rings true because we seem to make sense of the afterlife based on our experiences in the living world. On another level, the notion hints at the idea that love is at the heart of questions about the afterlife. Missing someone—whether a friend, spouse, lover, or family member—is perhaps largely why we fear death and why we mourn. And perhaps it is how we make sense of death, too. Antony announces, "I will be / A bridegroom in my death, and run into't / As to a lover's bed" (4.15.99–101). Certainly, he imagines that he couples with Cleopatra in death, but he also suggests that he marries death itself as his words echo those of Claudio in *Measure for Measure*:

> If I must die,
> I will encounter darkness as a bride,
> And hug it in mine arms. (3.1.81–2)

It is difficult *not* to interpret Antony's vision of death-as-reunion as pure fantasy, not only a desire for wish-fulfillment on his part but also a gesture toward the promise of love as immortal. On the one hand, Antony imagines that he and Cleopatra (and, by implication, also his human attendant Eros, playing an ambiguous role here as a third person in the re-coupling) will be happier than any of the dead they encounter in the underworld. On an abstract level, he imagines that Eros, that is, the abstract feeling of love, can carry on after death. It is a powerful fantasy, but it is one that tracks neither to early modern beliefs about the afterlife nor to the result for the other famous couple named in the scene: Dido and Aeneas. Early modern Protestant belief largely held that people were not reunited after death. John Woolton's *New Anatomy of Whole Man* (1576), for example, suggests that "because there shall be no mortality, marriage shall not be then needful by new procreation, to preserve and continue natures and substances."[42] In fact, the wedding rite that included the lines, "to have and to hold from this day forward, for better, for worse, [. . .] till death us depart"[43] in the post-Reformation period was taken to "reinforce the termination of marital vows after death."[44] Even if we take this play as referring solely to the pagan afterlife, Antony's fantasy relies on a surprising re-conceptualization of Virgil's *Aeneid.*

Antony's experience does not track cleanly to Virgil's archetype, and not solely in the sense that Antony—unlike Aeneas—chooses Cleopatra over his duty to Rome. In the ancient epic, Dido commits suicide after being abandoned by her lover but the couple does not reunite happily after death. Aeneas encounters Dido in the afterlife in the "Grieving Meadows," a location that the ancient poet describes this way:

> Here reside people that hardhearted Love, with his cruel
> corrosion,
> Wholly consumed. Tracks, traceless and secret, conceal them
> and myrtle
> Forests enclose them. For, even in death, anxiety's heartaches
> Fail to desert them. (6.442–5)[45]

This site for unrequited lovers seems far from the idyllic locale that Antony envisions. Virgil depicts Aeneas encountering Dido here, "fresh from her wound" (6.451). The hero attempts to assuage her and explain why he abandoned her, but

> She turned her back on him, stared at the ground, eyes fixed, her
> expression
> No more moved by these efforts at conversation than hard flint
> Slabs, or the marble face of the crags in Marpessus of Paros.
> She, in the end, made the break herself, full of hate, and took
> refuge
> Deep in the ghost-shadowed grove where her earlier husband,
> Sychaeus,
> Matches her cares with his own and whose love matches hers
> very fairly. (6.469–74)

This is not the only time that one of Shakespeare's characters miscasts Aeneas and Dido in a romantic light. In *The Merchant of Venice*, Lorenzo woos Jessica with depictions of lovers from antiquity including Jason and Medea *and* Troilus and Cressida *and* Pyramis and Thisbe, and he goes on to liken their night together to a time when:

> In such a night
> Stood Dido with a willow in her hand
> Upon the wild sea banks, and waft her love
> To come again to Carthage. (5.1.9–12)

Of all the candidates for ancient couples upon which to model a marriage, perhaps these are not the most compelling ones if you are wooing someone. But their inclusion in these plays is part of a persistent fantasy in Shakespeare that is also at the heart of love: that things will not resolve as they have in the past. That we can write our own destinies, that our own pasts are malleable as we re-characterize them in memory as foreshadowing positive outcomes. This is the "cruel optimism" that Lauren Berlant has argued is at the heart of desire, where

> when we talk about an object of desire, we are really talking about a cluster of promises we want someone or something to make to us and make possible for us. [. . .] That does not mean that they all feel optimistic: one might dread, for example, returning to a scene of hunger or longing or the slapstick reiteration of a lover or parent's typical misrecognition. But the surrender to the return to the scene where the object hovers in its potentialities is the operation of optimism as an affective form.[46]

Perhaps Shakespeare's re-telling of the story of Antony and Cleopatra opens a space for new fictions, including one where Aeneas and Dido somehow might have finally reconciled in this new space of the afterlife. This is the impulse to frame new experiences in such a way as to ornament previous experiences—re-characterizing them as learning opportunities, suggesting that we grew from them, encouraging us to imagine that former partners are happy now, or suggesting that we always should try to remember the good times.

This play's depictions of the afterlife thus add new dimension to David Scott Kastan's claim that Shakespeare delivers an experience outside of history: "the workings of his imagination are at least temporarily able to escape the constraints of the orthodoxies, even of the controversies, that defined his age."[47] In this play which itself is a fiction, in a pagan history whose religion would be a fiction to the early modern audience, Shakespeare seems to freely admit that the afterlife his characters imagine is a fiction, and this admission echoes early modern debates about whether individuals could know anything about what happens after death. Ideas about the afterlife were diverse and increasingly fractured during Shakespeare's time. As Peter Marshall notes, during the seventeenth century, "an increasing number of English religious radicals would be prepared to reject the very notion of a localized afterlife, to assert that Heaven and Hell were no more than spiritual states experienced in this life."[48]

Antony's suicide, his rush to join Cleopatra in the afterlife, is a botched attempt, a misguided show of valor. He is only wounded, and it is hard not to see the stunted drama as reflecting the failure of his fantasy of reunion. Indeed, a 2014 Globe Theatre production of the play generated unexpected laughs from the audience in the moment when Antony does not die from the self-inflicted wound. Clive Wood—the actor playing Antony in that production—seemed to go along with the audience's mood when he broke from the character's stern demeanor and the actor himself started laughing when his Antony learned the news that earlier word of Cleopatra's death was false. When we acknowledge the weight of fantasy required to shore up the fantasy of romance, the drama borders on farce.

Taking the afterlife as our focus in *Antony and Cleopatra* helps us see how the lovers' fantasies play with binary distinctions between past and present, between what happens before and after death. Antony learns that Cleopatra is in fact locked in her funeral monument because "She had a prophesying fear / Of what hath come to pass" (4.15.118–19). To send word to Antony that she had died, then, was not entirely false. "Belief," as Adam Phillips has remarked, "is a form of prophecy: it offers to tell you something about your future self."[49] Phillips' formulation works in the obverse, naturally, as prophecy shapes our present self, already molding ourselves to reflect the expectation of what is to come. Here, clearly, the prophecy of the dead lovers both predicts the ending that audiences expect and also tells Cleopatra something about her present self. Her love for Antony is intimately connected to death.

But death, while it will signal the end of this play, is not in Cleopatra's and Antony's minds the end of their love story. Both characters are deeply invested in the promise of reunion after death, and that future resurrection in a new world is not just pre-configured by a past coming together but more importantly offers a return to the past. Preparing to die, Cleopatra announces, "I am again for Cydnus / To meet Mark Antony" (5.2.224–5). As Ramie Targoff observes, Cleopatra projects her future self into "the location of their first encounter as if Cydnus were itself magically transposed to the afterlife, becoming a private Elysium that reflects their own personal history."[50]

To move forward into the "life to come" (as Macbeth describes the afterlife), the Egyptian queen will travel backward in time and into memory. Phillips is helpful again here, remarking of Hamlet's famous soliloquy on suicide, "one of the ways we bear the unknownness of the future is to treat it as though it was, in fact, the past; and as though the past was something we *did* know about".[51] Both Cleopatra and Antony hope for a future that resembles a familiar past but moreover they wish for a future capable of re-constituting the past in a way that obviates their love story's tragic end.

While Antony's death scene links closely to love and desire, Cleopatra's suicide even more overtly links dying with erotic fulfillment. The language where she will "die" from a bite from a "worm" offers sly puns that imply a phallic encounter that induces *la petite mort*—the "little death" of orgasm—thus exposing the close ties between her own sexualized demise and future commemoration. The "worm [. . .] that kills but pains not" is at once not deadly and sexual yet we are also told that "those that do die of it do seldom or never recover" (5.2.238–9, 5.2.242–3). Cleopatra declares, "I have / Immortal longings in me," pointing to her desire to die (and thereby enter an eternal space) and to the way her death will make her immortal in the remembrance of her among the living (5.2.275–6). The notion that her longings cannot die also suggests that they are powerful enough to carry on into the afterlife. In his final moments when he has managed to make his way to Cleopatra's tomb and share a final kiss, Antony declares, "Now my spirit is going; / I can no more" (4.16.60–1). "Spirit" is multivalent here, connoting his life force, his exiting ghost, and his sexual vitality. Thus, we can imagine these lines to imply that he has lost his ability to perform sexually but we can also interpret them to imply that his spirit is carrying over into the afterlife. In the case of Shakespeare's characters here, the loss of life on the physical plane propels forward energies of pure sexual desire and these energies are the fuel for the fantasy of an afterlife.

In the final lines of the play, Cleopatra fixates on reunion as an alternative outcome to the self-shattering effects of physical death. She says, "methinks I hear / Antony call. I see him rouse himself / To praise my noble act" (5.2.278–80). In her mind, Antony wakes from the sleep of death (or in the case of Atölyesi's production described at the start of this section, perhaps his ghost regards her with some urgency). Shortly after proclaiming, "Husband, I come," Cleopatra utters her final words, "What should I stay –" (5.2.282, 5.2.307). The moment leaves her—and us as the audience—in a curious state. Are we to interpret her death as simultaneous with sexual release? Did she intend to say more? We can interpret her final line as an act of self-scripting, of shaping her own story, especially when we acknowledge that "stay" in Shakespeare's time held a now obsolete meaning of "To cease speaking, break off one's discourse; to pause, stop or hesitate before speaking."

Like her exclamation, "Husband I come," "should I stay" places us in the eternal present, at the horizon of the conditional. After her death, she is described by Caesar this way:

> [. . .] she looks like sleep,
> As she would catch another Anthony
> In her strong toil of grace. (5.2.340–2)

The notion that she could "catch another Anthony" implies both that she is at the height of attractiveness in death and that a different incarnation of Antony awaits her in the afterlife. Stanley Wells invites us to view these lines as troubling the genre of the play, where this "tragedy ends, like romantic comedy, with the expectation of marriage."[52] The play's final moment, then, is the space of fictions, of possibilities. At the opening of the scene, Cleopatra announces that "My desolation does begin to make / A better life" (5.2.1–2). While the characters' afterlives are unknown to us—we are excluded from viewing what we have already heard Hamlet describe as that "something after death, / The undiscovered country from whose bourn / No traveller returns" (3.1.80–2)—we are left to imagine that perhaps there really is another Antony in another country, in another moment in time, and in a much longer narrative from which the living are excluded.

3

Dialogues with the Dead

Individuals living in Shakespeare's England were surrounded by the dead. As we saw in the previous chapter, the funeral monument functioned as a reminder of those who had passed, and Shakespeare underscores this dynamic by having several of his plays' crucial scenes take place in tombs. In Chapter 5, we will think about how individuals were memorialized in writing and how this also functioned to keep the dead in the company of the living. This chapter, though, focuses on imagined engagement with the dead in the form of a ghost. Undead spirits appear in Shakespeare's plays and serve a variety of purposes. In *Julius Caesar* and in *Richard III*, ghosts place guilt upon the living. In *Hamlet*, the spirit of the father incites a desire for revenge within the son. In *Cymbeline*, ghosts complain to Jupiter and deliver a prophecy. In *Macbeth*, they both place guilt upon the living and also grant a vision of the future in ways that generate insight into how ghosts disturb our understanding of normative temporality. Ghosts were common figures on the Renaissance stage, as well as in poetry and prose. They offered witnesses for those writers seeking to depict characters who could testify to the nature of the afterlife. For example, Barnebe Riche's *Greene's News Both From Heaven and Hell* (1593) was written from the first-person perspective of the ghost of the author Robert Greene (who, Riche claimed, delivered the manuscript to him). The speaker describes how he is first rejected at the gates of heaven by Saint Peter and then rejected from a fiery hell by Lucifer.

The question of how to stage ghosts provides interesting options for production companies and, in turn, gives way to multiple interpretations for the audience. On the early modern stage, actors would have used flour to whiten their faces when appearing as ghosts. More recent performances probably demonstrate less consistency in conventions used to signal the presence of the dead. The imaginative range is expanded further by the capabilities of the medium of film. For example, the 2009 *Hamlet* casts the same actor as King Hamlet and as Claudius.[1] Such a move raises new questions about the play. Were these brothers born as twins? Can their likeness explain Gertrude's ease in re-marrying?[2] Does hearing lines from the two different characters in the same voice lead us to identify shared inner qualities between King Hamlet and the brother who murdered him? This film version has the ghost appear and disappear in a single scene, utilizing the camera's varying point of view in order to call into question the veracity of Hamlet's vison. Productions of this play make crucial costuming decisions that influence our interpretation of the ghost. Dressing the spirit in armor in the 2009 Royal Shakespeare Company's film version implies that the king looks in the afterlife as he did at the moment of his death and suggests that he is still ready to do battle. Dressing the ghost in royal garb or in a business suit, as the 2000 film *Hamlet* does, can imply a spirit more somber and less combative, one that more resembles Hamlet's memory of a regal, stately, or sympathetic father. In that film, characters observe the ghost on a closed-circuit security camera which, in turn, suggests the ghost to be quite real.[3] Production decisions on the early modern stage and on the modern stage can further influence audience interpretations. Should the ghost emerge from the trapdoor in the stage, which would imply that it comes from hell? Would it be lowered from above? Would it come from the side of the stage, as mortal characters do? Such decisions raise questions about *where* the afterlife is located physically. In Christopher Marlowe's *Doctor Faustus*, the devil appears and remarks that "this is hell, nor am I out of it."[4] Such a statement troubles our sense of the boundaries between heaven or hell and our own earthly region, both in the limited space of the stage and in our larger cultural imagination.

What even are ghosts? Philippe Ariès observes that, when one imagines the afterlife, "the idea of infinite immortality is less important than the idea of an extension."[5] We see this across depictions of ghosts on Shakespeare's stage. Their presence raises questions about why they remain and what they want. If a ghost is an extension of a person's life, then we can think of one as an indication of unfinished business.

Ghosts are a sign of crisis, an echo. Ghosts are expressions of unresolved conflict. They might push for justice or demand revenge. They might be anchored to one particular location, a site of trauma. They might be limited to appearing only at night or in dreams. They might be known or unknown to those who witness them. They might be harbingers of the witness' own forthcoming transition to the afterlife. They might exist to prevent the death of the witness or to prevent further wrong in the world. They fulfill the fantasy that we will have an effect on the world and reassure us that unfinished business might be resolved. They might be demons. Or they might not be dead at all. Certainly, living characters are sometimes mistaken for ghosts in Shakespeare's work. We will see discussion of this in Chapter 4. For most Protestants in Reformation England, ghosts are a fiction. In Luke 16:26, Abraham describes a "great gulf" between the living and the dead "so that they which would pass from hence to you cannot: neither can they pass to us, that would come from hence." If we take the notion of visitations from the dead to be impossible, then ghosts must always stand in for something else.

Intriguingly, it is rare to encounter a female ghost in Shakespeare's work and in the larger canon of early modern theater. Frances Dolan's study of representations in literature and in archives finds "a dearth of female ghosts both before and after the Reformation, in continental Europe as well as in England."[6] Ann Jones and Peter Stallybrass suggest that one possible reason for this lack might be that much of the political, legal, and economic power belonged to men, who in turn are more likely to exert force from beyond the grave.[7] Dolan specifically suggests that in "Shakespeare's plays, the women who are dead have often completed their most important task, which is to give birth and die, or at the very least to die, and so have no unfinished business."[8] Not only do male ghosts appear with a will to exert force in the world but the power of the patriarchy also is performed on stage in the form of spectral presences that are unseen. Take, for example, the lingering presence of Portia's father in *The Merchant of Venice.* His ghost does not appear on stage, but his will (both in the sense of his desire and in the sense of his testamentary requirements) haunts his daughter in the form of the casket game that he has designed to determine her future husband.[9] What Jacques Derrida says of Hamlet's encounter with the ghost, "one never inherits without coming to terms with [*s'expliquer avec*] some specter," holds true for Portia, as well.[10] Her inheritance is both the wealth that will transfer to her husband *and* the control of her father over who will be her husband.

The Ghosts in *Julius Caesar*

Reinforcing an idea that we will see in *Richard III* and in *Macbeth*, a ghost signals disorder in the living world and the ramifications of past action in *Julius Caesar*. At first, the presence of ghosts functions as a symptom of the upset in the state. Later, the appearance of Caesar's ghost to one of his murderers emphasizes that the conspirator must live—or die—with what he has done.

Even before Caesar returns as a ghost, the boundary between the living and the dead becomes permeable in the play. This alerts us to the ways that some characters perceive the world is out of joint or in disorder when the senators conspire to usurp their ruler. Calpurnia tells Caesar about a series of "horrid sights" seen in public in Rome, including:

> A lioness hath whelpèd in the streets,
> And graves have yawned and yielded up their dead.
> Fierce fiery warriors fight upon the clouds,
> In ranks and squadrons and right form of war,
> Which drizzled blood upon the Capitol.
> The noise of battle hurtled in the air.
> Horses do neigh, and dying men did groan,
> And ghosts did shriek and squeal about the streets.
> O Caesar, these things are beyond all use,
> And I do fear them. (2.2.17–26)

We see here how ghosts are part of an inventory of elements that signal that the world has gone topsy-turvy. The lioness with her cubs in the streets of the city disturbs boundaries between human and animal, between civilized and wild. Calpurnia's description begins with the notion that gods are at war in the heavens, spilling blood. The "fiery warriors" could be interpreted as some divine combat or as personification of a lightning storm with heavy rain. In either case, this reinforces the blurring of categories and boundaries. Just as conflict between the gods has crossed over into the terrestrial realm of mortals, the restless dead have crossed back into the reality of the living. Animals, the living, and the dead cry out, implying such distress that it affects several realms. If we trust this description of the state of the city, it appears that the natural order has been upset. Caesar labels these as "predictions," connecting the crossing over of the dead into the world of the living with prophecy and the future (2.2.28). As we will see in this chapter, ghosts are surprisingly as much about the future as they are about the past. As Stanley Wells notes, Caesar's own ghost will be "essentially premonitory rather than vengeful."[11]

A breakdown in the boundary between the dead and the living foreshadows more conflict to come. The murder of Julius Caesar can be seen as a logical consequence or an additional symptom of the disturbances of the boundaries between the dead and living. In Mark Antony's funeral oration, he states that "My heart is in the coffin there with Caesar, / And I must pause till it come back to me" (3.2.107–8). It is a statement of grief that functions in a way similar to Freud's notion of the ego-disturbing effects of mourning, where the loss of the beloved object is experienced as a loss of part of oneself. While perhaps inauthentic and ultimately cynical, Mark Antony's expression of grief is also very early modern in character, as friends were thought to share "one heart." The notion itself was inherited from writers in classical antiquity such as Cicero who claimed friends to be of "one mind," and so it is not surprising to find it here in this play with its ancient setting.[12] Within his classical treatise on friendship, the Roman writer Cicero reiterates the notion of the true friend as "another self" from Aristotle because it captures the way a man "looks for another whose mind he may, so to speak, mingle with his own so as to turn the two into one."[13] Bacon refers to the ancient wisdom in his essay "Of Friendship" when he asserts that "a friend is another himself."[14] The concept of two friends sharing one heart would be familiar to playgoers and, they would sympathize with the trauma experienced when such a bond is broken. As Mark Antony laments his living heart trapped in the coffin with his friend, audiences would also see one more instance of the problematically crossed boundaries that saturate this play.

The ghost of Caesar confronts Brutus when he is taking a respite from the battlefield. The arrival of the specter is telegraphed when Brutus remarks "How ill this taper burns," as the suddenly waning flame of the candle perhaps points to a disturbance in the physical world. At first he believes the arriving spirit to be an illusion as it could be "the weakness of mine eyes / That shapes this monstrous apparition" (4.2.327–8). Perhaps fearing the evil intent implied by the "monstrous" appearance of the visitor, he then asks the question that early modern audience members would also ask of any ghost: "Art thou any thing? / Art thou some god, some angel, or some devil, / That mak'st my blood cold and my hair to stare?" (4.2.329–31). He then demands that the thing explain itself, "Speak to me what thou art" (4.2.332) We hear resonances of *Hamlet* here where the mortal questions the nature of the spirit and then makes demand that it speak.

While Brutus has tried to separate himself from the ghost by demanding affirmation of the intruder's alien quality, the ghost replies with an assertion of its close kinship with the man. We have an evocative moment when the spirit announces that it is "Thy evil spirit, Brutus" (4.2.333). The stage directions specify "*Enter the Ghost of Caesar*," so we know this is Caesar's spirit and that it would be played by the same actor. However, the status of these men as friends in life, where the friend is "another self," sets up the two men as foils here. The ghost tells Brutus that it has come to "To tell thee thou shalt see me at Philippi" (4.2.335). Once more, the ghost demonstrates ties to the future and to prophecy. His curiously gnomic utterance lacks any kind of rage and does not attempt to intervene in forthcoming events. While this ghost represents the future to Brutus, it represents history to later audiences. If we understand the figure of the ghost to signify inevitability, then we can read Brutus' reply, "Why, I will see thee at Philippi then," as tinged with resignation (4.2.337). When the ghost exits, Brutus announces, "Now I have taken heart, thou vanishes. / Ill spirit, I would hold more talk with thee" (4.2.338–9). Like Hamlet, Brutus senses that the ghost has more to tell him and longs for prolonged interaction with the entity despite the fact that he associates it with ill will. At the same time, the ghost has stated to Brutus that he is "*thy* evil spirit" (my emphasis). Thus, to converse with it would be to uncover self-knowledge.

The ghost's effect is not only to rattle Brutus here in his sleeping chamber but to undermine all of those who side with Brutus. Hearing of the suicide of Titinius, Brutus exclaims, "O Julius Caesar, though art mighty yet. / Thy spirit walks abroad, and turns our swords / In our own proper entrails" (5.3.93–5). We can interpret these lines to mean that the deaths are caused both by the guilt of having killed Julius Caesar and by the power of his legacy that drives the opposition. Brutus tells Volumnius, "The ghost of Caesar hath appeared to me / Two several times by night—at Sardis once, / And this last night, here in Philippi fields" (5.5.17–19). He concludes, "I know my hour is come" (5.5.20). Brutus further concedes, "Our enemies have beat us to the pit," using a term ("pit") that denotes how they have been beaten to the core and how they have been ushered to their destinations in hell (5.5.23).[15]

The presence of a ghost signifies that death itself is near. In this case, the ghost of the friend foreshadows Brutus' own death. The loyal friend Antony mourns the loss of his own heart in Caesar, but we know that this grief will pass and we see how he deploys it to rouse the spirits of the living. By contrast, the disloyal friend Brutus encounters his own spirit in Caesar and understands it as a sign of his demise and the dispiriting of those troops aligned with the conspirators.

Richard III and the Ambiguous Space of the Ghostly Realm

Richard III features the largest number of ghosts in any of Shakespeare's plays. In some ways, it is unsurprising that a history play—with its central concern being how past events came to occur and how they might explain subsequent history—would feature ghosts.[16] In 5.4, the stage is populated by Richard's victims, eleven people whom he has killed or arranged to have killed. The group includes Henry VI and his widow (also Richard's wife) Anne; the two young princes; and Richard's sometime allies Buckingham and Hastings. Hester Lees-Jeffries aptly notes that this play's "ghosts are not characters, primarily, but devices to jog the memory, the audience's as well as Richard's."[17] Her point helps us see how figures from the afterlife both shockingly interrupt storylines and also serve the needs of narrative continuity.

The ghosts serve another important role by emphasizing how two locations or spaces, that of the afterlife and that of the stage, overlap when the dead appear among the living. In the space of this single scene, the dead alternatively address both Richard and Richmond, who are in different places. The ghost of Prince Edward says to

Richard, "Let me sit heavy on thy soul tomorrow," and then to Richmond, "the wrongèd souls / Of butchered princes fight on your behalf" (5.5.71, 5.5.75–6). The ghost of Henry VI urges Richard to "Despair and die" while he commands Richmond to "Live and flourish!" (5.5.80, 5.5.84). The ghost of Queen Anne promises to use her supernatural influence to fill Richard's "sleep with perturbations" and to guarantee Richmond "a quiet sleep" (5.5.115, 5.5.118). It is not surprising that the villain's victims would work to ensure his defeat. What is startling here is the ambiguity surrounding their location. This scene exemplifies the claims by scholars Peter Buse and Andrew Stott, that ghosts can be understood as "standing in defiance of binary oppositions such as presence and absence, body and spirit, past and present, life and death."[18]

While the scene shares qualities with other depictions of ghosts that we have seen in Shakespeare's work, it presents a new level of complexity in terms of where and when the afterlife resides. On one level, we see these ghosts as figures of a conflicted past whose demand for justice has influence on the present. On another level, we recognize them as being in two places at once. How exactly do ghosts visit the living? At one point, all of the ghosts speak to Richmond in unison:

> Awake, and think our wrongs in Richard's bosom
> Will conquer him. Awake, and win the day! (5.5.98–9)

Are these ghosts all in the same place? Are they in the afterlife? Are they simultaneously in two places at once? Are they in some third space that touches the rooms of both these leaders? Do they inhabit the same moment in time as the living? Do these visitations take place sequentially somehow? We might be tempted to answer, "yes *and* no" to several of these questions. Can it be both? These seeming paradoxes become possibilities because, as Carlos Eire puts it, "to imagine eternity is to venture beyond the world of sense experience, to ponder the unimaginable, to contemplate the ultimate."[19] The notion of the afterlife fuels imaginative expression in the theater. Because "eternity is beyond comprehension, but not beyond the mind's grasp," the scene can make sense even if we cannot explain how it would operate in actuality.[20] That is, we understand these spirits to exist in a space that is not actually the space in which we witness them, even if we cannot comprehend how that can be possible.

The ghost-realm reveals itself as a *heterotopia* in this scene. As Michel Foucault defines the term, a heterotopia is a particular type of space that "is capable of juxtaposing in a single real place several spaces, several sites that are in themselves incompatible."[21] The term itself combines two ancient Greek words: *hetero-*, a prefix which means "different" or "other," and *topos*, which means "space." We recognize unusual spatial dynamics in the scene from *Richard III* because the two men's sleeping quarters cannot be so close to each other as to appear on a single stage. The co-location of the mortal characters, though, signifies their parallel but opposing experiences of the dead and the simultaneity of the action. While Shakespeare breaks Aristotle's three unities in many of his plays, this instance constitutes a particularly radical departure from the ancient rules. Aristotle states that a play should have a single storyline without digression, should have a stage that is consistently the same location, and should take place within twenty-four hours. Here, we clearly see distinct pairs of places (the two bedchambers as well as the world of the living and the world of the dead), and two different zones of time (the linear, progressive, finite world of humans and the eternal, ageless, non-cyclical world of the dead). Intriguingly, the realm of the dead and the realm of the living seem impossibly close. We might also add that, if the ghosts appear to the men in their dreams, given that Richard relates "Methought the souls of all that I had murdered / Came to my tent" (5.5.158–89), then the space of the sleeping mind should also be incompatible with the external space of the playgoer. In fact, Foucault names the theater as an example of a heterotopia, as "the theatre brings onto the rectangle of the stage, one after the other, a whole series of places that are foreign to one another."[22] The scene is that much more complex, then, as the audience has an ambiguous relationship to the spectral visitors who seem to invade not only the physical locations of the sleeping men but their dreaming minds as well.

Foucault adds to his discussion that the peculiar spaces traced by his analysis also function as "heterochronies" or "slices of time," where multiple time periods might appear to occur simultaneously. In other plays, we have seen ghosts tied to prophecy, and here they are determined to influence the future. Moreover, here in *Richard III*, we witness a flashpoint for the propensity of the ghost to trouble our sense of time. "The ghost," Roger Lockhart argues, "intersects and divides contemporaneity with a double gesture that invaginates the past and future into the present."[23] The spirits in *Richard III* represent Richard's past come back to haunt him, as well as the weight of the past on future outcomes. Just as the presence of ghosts in *Julius Caesar* was a component of a larger set of breakdowns in binary categories, their presence in *Richard III* signals a disturbance in the normal order of the state. The presence of ghosts also reminds playgoers that every historical character on stage is already dead by the century in which the play is performed. Yet they are still alive in the cultural memory and are revived in the flesh-and-blood performance. Such is the work of the history play, perhaps. It revives the past for a moment to recall the events that led to the present and also that shape the history to come.

Hamlet and the Specter of Memory

As we have seen in this volume thus far, discussion of the afterlife inevitably returns us to *Hamlet.* While *Richard III* features the most ghosts in a play by Shakespeare, *Hamlet* uses the word "ghost" the most times. And, like the figure of Revenge who appears on stage alongside the ghost of Don Andrea in Thomas Kyd's *The Spanish Tragedy* (1587), the ghost in *Hamlet* seems to be an omniscient observer of the action and a driver of the narrative.

Like Brutus when confronted by the ghost of Caesar, Hamlet, and other characters at first do not know what to make of King Hamlet's return from the dead. During the initial appearance of the spirit, Bernardo recognizes it as "In the same figure like the King that's dead," but this does not necessarily mean that it is the spirit of the dead man (1.1.39). Martin Luther warned, "whatever spirits go about, making a noise, screaming, complaining, or seeking help, are truly the work of the devil."[24] Later, when Hamlet begins to follow the ghost, Horatio wonders if it could be a deceiver who might lure him away and "assume some other horrible form / Which might deprive your sovereignty of reason / And draw you into madness?" (1.4.53–5). If one believes that ghosts cause insanity, Luther's and Horatio's claims provide strong support for Hamlet's madness not being feigned. Horatio does seem to be a knowledgeable source. Marcellus thinks that this friend of Hamlet from the university should approach it, "Thou art a scholar—speak to it, Horatio" (1.1.40). However, after encountering the ghost, Hamlet will tell his friend that "There are more things in heaven and earth, Horatio, / Than are dreamt of in our philosophy" (1.5.168–9). This unknowability of the afterlife is then tied to madness in the famous soliloquy when Hamlet says that the "undiscovered country" located after death "puzzles the will" (3.1.82). In this term "will," we hear how contemplation of the afterlife both undermines the prince's reason and his decisiveness. Arthur Kinney notes the "sharp disjunction between Hamlet's studies at Wittenberg and events in Denmark," resulting in a situation where the "ghost's story and command have undone him because they refuse to square with anything he has learned."[25] This dovetails with the notion of the afterlife as unknowable and opens us to competing explanations for Hamlet's seeming madness.

The idea that the entity claiming to be King Hamlet's ghost resides in Purgatory points to an early conception of the afterlife that emerged in the medieval period and was subsequently called into question during the Protestant Reformation. Purgatory emerged as a concept in the twelfth century, and it was the sale of "indulgences" that could hurry one's passage through it that incentivized Luther to challenge the church (and in turn initiate the debates at the heart of the Reformation). Scholars debate the exact date of the introduction of the idea of Purgatory. Jacques Le Goff's major study places it toward the end of the twelfth century, though he admits that "the idea that there is another place above Hell in the other world" began to emerge in embryonic form as early as the sixth century before it coalesced into the discrete concept of Purgatory.[26] While denial of the existence of Purgatory was central to the rejection of Catholicism, Mullaney reminds us that "in the course of the English Reformation, the English people did not become indifferent to the fates of their predecessors; they did not cease to feel the loss of loved ones or to mourn their passing in public and private rituals and in other, less codified expressions of grief."[27] This claim dovetails with Greenblatt's observation that Purgatory "provided a powerful method of negotiating with the dead, or, rather, with those who were at once dead and yes, since they could still speak, appeal, and appall, not completely dead."[28] Though the Reformation may have dismissed Purgatory, neither could its long history be elided nor its symbolic power assuage longing to connect with the dead. Because one day's suffering on

Earth was equivalent to one thousand years in Purgatory, indulgences could be calculated with a very precise accounting system.[29] Like the ghosts who can inhabit ambiguous zones of time and place on the stage in *Richard III*, the ghost of Hamlet's father may also inhabit a peculiar locus of space/time.

In *Hamlet*, the specter represents the powerful force of memory, both personal memory and cultural memory. The ghost transmits personal memory because the son should emulate the father, an idea we see emphasized in the 1996 *Hamlet* (dir. Branagh) where close-up shots emphasize the matching blue eyes of the son and father.[30] The ghost's injunction to "Remember me" demands both that Hamlet recall the past and that he take actions that will shape the future. The playwright thus "transforms a revenge tragedy into a play of cathartic remembering" because many of the over 4,000 lines of this play are devoted to Hamlet struggling to recall and honor his dead father.[31] The Prince's insistence on wearing black longer than others do, even before he learns of the ghost, underscores his propensity to dwell in the past and to follow appropriate ritual for honoring the dead. Hester Lees-Jeffries observes that "it is when such anxieties are focused around questions of *how* to remember the dead that it is most apparent that memory and remembering are not primarily about the past, but about the future."[32] The question of appropriate forms of mourning does not only appear here, of course. Feste's jest that Olivia should not mourn her brother if he is in heaven is another memorable instance where a character possibly engages in overindulgent mourning. Roland Barthes, in the journal in which he documented how he coped with the death of his mother, identifies in the mourning process "an acute phase of narcissism" when confronted with "the death of the loved being."[33] Hamlet insists on wearing black, sighing, and weeping longer than others do after his father's death (1.2.76–86). His mother and his uncle suggest that he is being overly dramatic. However, we can interpret this self-indulgent behavior to reflect an impulse to keep the father alive in his memory and as foreshadowing for the otherworldly return of this father's spirit.

The ghost of a parent on stage would resonate for an early modern audience not only as a representation of the previous generation, but also as a representation of the previous religious mindset. Frances Dolan suggests that "Catholicism was the undead of Post-Reformation

English culture," and certainly this spirit in *Hamlet* emphasizes that the past lingers in personal and cultural memory.[34] Stephen Greenblatt argues that Shakespeare was "haunted by the spirit of his Catholic father."[35] We do not know what Shakespeare believed, but we do know that he integrated and responded to debates about religious belief within his work. When we see representations of the past in *Hamlet*, they appear as a ghost or a skull encountering on the periphery of the social world. These are reminders for the characters not only that they too will die but also that the past lingers on the outskirts of the present. In this play, the ghost signifies how the presence of unresolved issues of the past—whether these are family dynamics, political conflicts, or theological concerns—can disrupt the stability of interpersonal and courtly relations, as well as undermine the veracity of religious beliefs.

The ghost reappears to Hamlet when he confronts his mother in 3.4. Gertrude does not see the ghost, just as Lady Macbeth does not see the ghost of Banquo. Has Hamlet gone mad at this point and imagines this second sighting of the ghost? Or is there a reason that his father would only appear to him? Hamlet confronts his mother in her closet, or dressing room, shortly after Claudius has reacted to the *Murder of Gonzago*. The ghost of King Hamlet appears and counsels,

> Do not forget. This visitation
> Is but to whet thy almost blunted purpose.
> But look, amazement on thy mother sits.
> O, step between her and her fighting soul.
> Conceit in weakest bodies strongest works.
> Speak to her, Hamlet. (3.4.100–5)

The ghost demands specific action, functioning as a director for Hamlet as an actor and nudging his son to engage in dialogue. He is also a fellow actor, in the sense that Bert O. States captures nicely in his discussion of this play, "we speak of actors as feeding each other lines, but it would be more accurate to say that they feed each other character."[36] Certainly, this claim holds true for a father chiding his son in this treatment of Gertrude. In Doran's film version described here earlier, Hamlet (played by David Tennant) confronts his mother in a dressing room that has a large mirror. The careful cinematography showcases how the ghost is present only when we see

Figure 3.1. An unruly Hamlet no longer reflects his father's desire to leave Gertrude out of the whole affair. *Hamlet* (Dir. Doran, 2009).

the scene from Hamlet's point of view and from the objective view from the camera. When the perspective shifts to that Gertrude, the room is empty. A shattered mirror in the scene comes to symbolize how Hamlet has departed from his father's wishes (Figure 3.1).

Productions of *Hamlet*, both on stage and on screen, have experimented with a wide range of ways to depict the ghost. For example, some productions cast the same actor to play King Hamlet, the First Player, and one of the Gravediggers. The decision invites us to understand Hamlet's connection to the aging actor (who the young prince asks to recite a speech depicting a mourning mother and an avenging son) and to a man whose occupation is focused on death. Devotees of Shakespeare have also sought to locate the playwright's own experience of mourning in the play. They take the fact that Shakespeare's son who died was named Hamnet to indicate a deeply personal connection to this play. A probably apocryphal story holds that Shakespeare played King Hamlet at one time. Whatever the performative choices and whatever the biographical connection, the ghost in *Hamlet* clearly has vital purchase on memory; ranging from Hamlet's personal memory to our cultural memory, to perhaps Shakespeare's own memory.

Spectral Interventions in *Cymbeline*

Consistent with the visitation of ghosts upon the sleeping in *Richard III* or the nocturnal visitation in *Julius Caesar* and *Hamlet*, the arrival of spirits in *Cymbeline* occurs while Posthumus sleeps. In her study of early modern depictions of ghosts, Michelle O'Callaghan finds that these entities "are, by their nature, nocturnal visitors, habitually appearing to the living at the point of sleep or in a dream"; one reason for this might be that "like dreams, ghosts are cryptic both in the content for their messages and in their origins."[37] Knowing the close kinship between sleep and death in the early modern imagination, we might also imagine that sleep puts one closer to the supernatural world of the afterlife. In *Richard III*, it seemed as if the ghosts had entered the minds of the dreamers. Here, their interaction is largely with each other and with the god Jupiter. Nonetheless, these figures from the sleeper's past will influence his future. In fact, they even more concretely break down boundaries between the afterlife and the realm of the living when they leave him a tablet inscribed with his fortune.

The apparitions in this play include Posthumus Leonatus' father, who appears as "*an old man, attired like a warrior*;" he appears "*leading in his hand an ancient matron, his wife, and mother to Posthumus*" (s.d.). The father and mother are followed by the deceased brothers of Posthumus Leonatus, "*with wounds as they died in the wars*" (s.d.). It is interesting that the men come dressed for battle, as if connoting their willingness to fight for their relative. It is also interesting to note that all the ghosts seem to be the age they were when they passed on, with the brothers still showing their wounds from which they died. Perhaps the parents even continued to age after death. The young man's father died fighting in battle for Cymbeline, and his mother seems to have died in childbirth perhaps related to her "ancient" age at the time. Such representations would seem particularly significant to early modern playgoers, many of whom would have believed that people had young, healthy bodies in the afterlife. The stage directions tell us, "*They circle Posthumus Leonatus round, as he lies sleeping*" (s.d.). Rather than appear to enter the sleeper's dreams, as the ghosts seem to do in the case of the two combatants in *Richard III*, these spirits seem to have little interest in communicating directly with the youth.

The father addresses Jupiter, who is not yet present on stage. He pleads, "No more, thou thunder-master, show / Thy spite on mortal flies," and we hear an echo of *King Lear* here where boys' treatment of flies helped explain how gods relate to humans (5.5.124–5). We also hear an echo of *The Merchant of Venice*, where Gratiano wishes his wife were dead so that she could entreat God to save Antonio. Here in *Cymbeline*, the ghost expresses regret that he was not present to raise his son as he died while the baby was still in the womb. The child is named "Posthumus," in part, because he was born after his mother's death. The mother relates how "Lucina lent not me her aid, / But took me in my throes, / That from me was Posthumus ripped (5.5.137–9). Here we see another reference to the gods' whimsy as the Roman goddess of childbirth does not allow the mother to survive to see her baby born. The ways in which the ghosts each take turns briefly telling their tales of woe might remind some playgoers of the series of spectral speakers in the popular collection of poems entitled *Mirror for Magistrates* (1574). Indeed, the *Mirror for Magistrates* "set the pattern for ghost narratives for subsequent writers in the sixteenth and seventeenth centuries."[38] The need for ghosts to tell their stories—and especially the mother's articulated regret in this scene—provides support for Adam Phillips' claim that, because "we have grossly overrated the significance of our own deaths," we want to know both when we will die and what long-term effects our lives will have on others after we are gone.[39] The ghosts proclaim Posthumus "great Sicilius' heir" and a "fruitful object [...] / In the eye of Innogen" (5.5.145., 5.5.149–50). As Lees-Jeffries pointed out regarding *Richard III*, ghosts sometimes serve to jog the memories of audience members and here they provided a helpful through-line for this play with its labyrinthine plot. The ghosts then complain to Jupiter to "Take off his miseries" and to "Help" Posthumus (5.5.181, 5.5.185).

The notion that the dead "appeal" to Jupiter reverses the medieval idea that the living should pray to affect the conditions of the dead. When the god descends to the stage, "*The ghosts fall on their knees*" (s.d.). Jupiter addresses the family members as "you petty spirits of region low," admonishing them for their complaints and dismissing them with

> [. . .] How dare you ghosts
> Accuse the thunderer, whose bolt, you know,
> Sky-planted, batters all rebelling coasts?
> Poor shadows of Elysium, hence, and rest
> Upon your never-withering banks of flowers (5.5.187–92)

They are at once "poor shadows," recalling Macbeth's description of the living as a "poor player" and "walking shadow," and they also inhabit a blissful environ that is "never-withering." It is a markedly reassuring version of the afterlife. Jupiter then tells them to "Be content" because

> Your low-laid son our godhead will uplift.
> His comforts thrive, his trials well are spent.
> Our Jovial star reigned at his birth, and in
> Our temple was he married. (5.5.197–200)

The multilayered pantheons and temporalities here match the bricolage of plays and plots that circulate in *Cymbeline*. Strikingly, the play achieves what Carolyn Dinshaw describes as "the possibility of a fuller, denser, more crowded *now* that all sorts of theorists tell us is extant but that often eludes our temporal grasp."[40] Upon witnessing a Greco-Roman deity blessing the fortunes of an individual on the early modern stage, some audience members might recognize a nod to Geoffrey Whitney's *Choice of Emblems* (1586), which describes Jove blessing the early modern poet Philip Sidney's birth. The god in this scene quiets the ghosts who lament the past before he prophesizes the future. In fact, his instructions to them resemble stage directions:

> Rise, and fade.
> He shall be lord of Lady Innogen,
> And happier much by his affliction made.
> This tablet lay upon his breast, wherein
> Our pleasure his full fortune doth confine.
> And so, away. (5.5.20–5)

The tablet suggests a permeability between the world of the dead and that of the living. Posthumus' very name points to his connection to the dead, and this scene makes palpable that connection. As we saw in *Richard III* and in *Julius Caesar*, to be close to the dead involves a peculiar collapse of the past and the future. As we see these ghosts associated with influencing events to come and with delivering prophecies, it becomes clear why Adam Phillips asserts that "[t]he fact of death has made us addicted to prophecy, and to its secular equivalent, predictability; and therefore to a strange relationship to time."[41] Even in their eerie intangibility, ghosts make corporeal the grip that the past possesses on the present and the predicting power of the past upon the future. The curious temporality of the afterlife—eternal, ever-present—offers a useful heuristic device for understanding how past, present, and future collapse on the stage.

Ghostly Temporality in *Macbeth*

While the largest number of ghosts appears in *Richard III* and while the most instances of the word "ghost" appear in *Hamlet*, arguably the most familiar representation among Shakespeare's ghosts occurs in *Macbeth.* The return of Banquo to torment the friend who betrayed him is an iconic moment for secondary school students in the United States and for the broader public who knows this often-performed play. As we saw earlier in the case of *Julius Caesar*, ghosts are more complex than simple manifestations of characters' guilty consciences. Of course, there is certainly plenty of culpability brimming over in this play. *Macbeth* is, among other things, a series of highly memorable and highly dramatic displays of psyches racked with guilt—from Macbeth's imagining the murder weapon declaring, "Is this a dagger which I see before me" to Lady Macbeth rubbing her hands and exclaiming, "Out, damned spot; out, I say" (2.1.33, 5.1.33). As familiar as these moments may be, an equally memorable instance of the tortured mind on stage is the appearance of Banquo's ghost before Macbeth at a dinner banquet.

The stage directions, "*Enter the Ghost of Banquo, and sits in Macbeth's place*" urge us not to dismiss this entity as one wholly imagined by the protagonist (s.d.). Macbeth describes him as a "mockery," a term which implies simultaneously how he mocks human form and how he mocks Macbeth for his cowardly and dishonest deeds (3.4.106). The intrusion of the spirit of Banquo upon the dinner gathering and his placement in Macbeth's chair is a particularly charged moment. At its most basic level, this supernatural presence disturbs Macbeth because he now has nowhere to sit. On another level, the ghost's position emblematizes the price that Macbeth has paid by murdering his friend in order to achieve a prominent place at the table of Scottish nobility. This ghost renders visible one of the central tensions in *Macbeth:* the supernaturally inspired murders have upset normative lines of succession. The natural order would place Duncan at this table. It would also place Banquo, as the father of the future rulers, in a prominent physical place within this group. Yet, even in this complex matrix of representations, Shakespeare has simplified the issues of interrupted succession at work in the actual events upon which the play is based. The historical Banquo was one of the co-conspirators to usurp the king. Because Banquo was an ancestor of King James, he receives a much rosier characterization in the play. Shakespeare omits his historical role as a co-conspirator in the murder of King Duncan. Playgoers are thus set up to perceive this particular Banquo as an innocent victim and his ghost as a force for justice. At the same time, his taking Macbeth's seat at the table nevertheless indicates the character's historical counterpart (albeit in displaced form) as a usurper.

The banquet, like the rest of the play, is a site of disturbed temporality. Macbeth, at the urging of prophecy, has rushed his succession to the throne. While the present constitutes a hurried moment of crisis in the play, the audience would view the staged events as a distant past, even if a somewhat fictionalized version of those past events. From the perspective of Shakespeare's audience, these characters *are* ghosts in the sense that these future descendants of Banquo have already died by the time *Macbeth* premieres. Theater is already a space of repetition and of resurrection.

We learn early on that the world of this play is one that troubles normative temporality. That is, *Macbeth* is concerned with how time itself overlaps or feels "out of joint," to borrow a phrase from *Hamlet*, when living individuals interact with the supernatural. In 1.3, Banquo queries the witches, "If you can look into the seeds of time / And say which grain will grow and which will not" (1.3.56–7). As Christine Varnado notes, "the 'seeds of time' are, from Banquo's perspective, in the future."[42] Given this, Varnado further proposes that "time contains multiple, quantum possibilities in which some seeds of possible futures will grow, and others will not."[43] In the first act of the play, the witches proclaim, "All hail, Macbeth, that shalt be king hereafter!" (1.3.48).

He will certainly be king, but note the nearness of the term "king" to "hereafter." The *Oxford English Dictionary* traces the association of the word "hereafter" with the afterlife or "the world to come," back to the fourteenth century. The line, then, implies that Macbeth's ascension to king will accelerate his progress toward the hereafter. Once again, we find that the living world offers a pale mirror of the afterlife. The murder of Duncan leaves Macbeth wondering about "the life to come" (1.7.7). The phrase articulates his narrow focus on the next stage of his life, and it reveals his inability to see how quickly he rushes toward "the world to come" as well.

The encounter with the witches, that supernatural driver of the play's narrative, is also an encounter with the afterlife. When asked by Macbeth, Lennox reports that he did not see the weird sisters. This underscores the women's supernatural abilities, which include the capacity to vanish just as apparitions and ghosts can. Macbeth later exclaims "And damned all those that trust them," emphasizing his own fate to be damned to hell (4.1.155). In the disturbing scenes with the witches where Macbeth demands deeper engagement with the dark supernatural, it is easy to see why Ewan Fernie announces him "the Bard's most demonic figure" and asserts that "Macbeth is Shakespeare's Faustus."[44] Death looms in Macbeth's future, as it does for so many characters in the tragedies. Yet the boundary between the dead and the living blurs in this play. The blood that Lady Macbeth imagines she cannot wash from her hands reminds us that the dead, especially the murdered, linger in our memories as well.

Francis Beaumont's later play *The Knight of the Burning Pestle* (1607), a highly meta-theatrical comedy, features a scene that closely recalls the banquet scene in *Macbeth.* A character named Jasper pretends to be a ghost and describes how he will haunt a merchant. The stage directions describe Jasper's face "mealed," meaning that it is covered with flour, and he threatens the merchant thus:

> And never shalt though sit, or be alone
> In any place, but I will visit thee
> With ghastly looks, and put into thy mind
> The great offences which thou didst to me.
> When thou are at thy table with thy friends,
> Merry in heart, and filled with swelling wine,
> I'll come in the midst of all thy pride and mirth,

> Invisible to all men but thyself,
> And whisper such a sad tale in thine ear
> Shall make thee let the cup fall from thy hand,
> And stand as mute and pale as Death itself. (5.18–28)[45]

The lines from Beaumont's play underscore the dialectical relationship between the living and the dead. *The Knight of the Burning Pestle* contains a host of references to other plays with which early modern audience members would be familiar. *Macbeth* was written only a year earlier and thus playgoers would recognize, as Raphael Lyne puts it, "the ghost of Banquo's ghost" in this scene.[46] As a literary text that imitates other literary texts, Beaumont's play revives Banquo as much as it revives Shakespeare. In this scene, we see the familiar dynamic where we need the dead to emphasize to us that we are alive. At the same time, this scene (like many of Shakespeare's scenes that we have encountered thus far) dramatizes how thinking too much on death brings us closer to it. This instance of *memento mori* sets up the dead man as a counterpart to the living one, a figure who demands self-reflection.

This formulation of the ghost as a figure who reflects and demands reflection in *The Knight of the Burning Pestle* explains why Banquo will carry a mirror when he reappears later in *Macbeth*. With the stage direction "*A show of eight kings, the last with a glass in his hand; and Banquo*" (s.d.), we are alerted to the theatrical qualities, or "show," that the supernatural promises in stage productions. This parade of ghosts evinces how, as Simon Palfrey puts it nicely, the witches "scramble all temporality, all succession, so much so that they render the 'future' a thing of recollection."[47] There were eight Stuart kings of Scotland before the birth Mary, Queen of Scots (the mother of King James). The mirror thus could be added to a series of "particular moments of collapse—the collapse of past, present, and future into a single instant" that Heather Love has recently traced throughout the play.[48] In the *Mirror for Magistrates*, ghosts "explicitly function as mirrors" as they offer to those viewing them either positive or negative models of behavior.[49] It is, of course, too late for Macbeth but not too late for playgoers who seek a lesson from the play.[50] Banquo's ghost and the mirror he carriers reflect the destined line of kings and also the wrongness of disturbing that line of succession.

When Macbeth confronts the ghost during the banquet, we see once again the desire among the living to speak with visiting spirits. Just as Hamlet and Brutus longed for more discourse with the dead, Macbeth wishes that the ghost would do more than gesture physically:

> If thou canst nod, speak too!
> If charnel-houses and our graves must send
> Those that we bury back, our monuments
> Shall be the maws of kites. (3.4.69–72)

Here we see an example of how Shakespeare embeds stage directions in dialogue rather than stating them as such. The ghost has clearly nodded to Macbeth, and the gesture signifies that the dead man has come with the intent of provoking him. In these lines, Macbeth worries about the larger implications of the dead returning to the world of the living. Humans will have no reason to build funereal monuments if the dead will simply evacuate such edifices. Instead, the dead will reside in the mouths and stomachs of scavenger birds, who will eat their reanimated bodies. As Catherine Stevens puts it, "the ghost is transgressive, its ontology rendering it resistant to the boundaries that delineate oppositional categories such as life and death."[51] In addition to breaking down the expected binary between the silent tombs of the dead and the animated world of the living, the return of Banquo threatens the logics of legacy. Within the natural order, one generation dies to give way to the next generation. The return of this particular man reverses the expected dynamics of generational succession, and more specifically, the return of this man threatens the possibility of Macbeth possessing a positive legacy.

Once more, we see staged the desire for the ghost to speak. When Stephen Greenblatt famously remarked that the project of his scholarship was driven by "the desire to speak with the dead," he implied that he wanted to place himself in conversation about ideas from the past and learn more about those who lived in the early modern period.[52] Among these figures from the past, we see this same impulse to uncover the secrets held by the dead. Greenblatt, too, sees this desire dwelling among characters who encounter ghosts because their "collective impulse is not to flee from and not even simply ward off the weird apparition, but rather to approach and find out what it is and what it wants."[53] Ghosts rarely yield their secrets, though. When the phantom of Banquo will not speak, we witness Macbeth lash out and demand that it leave:

> Avaunt, and quit my sight! Let the earth hide thee.
> Thy bones are marrowless, thy blood is cold.
> Thou hast no speculation in those eyes
> Which thou dost glare with. (3.4.92–5)

He desires a return to the natural order. The dead should be in tombs, not terrifying the living and providing fodder for birds. Bones without marrow should not support locomotion, and un-reflecting eyes should not see. Macbeth longs for a return to stable categories and binary differences:

> What man dare, I dare.
> Approach thou like the ruggèd Russian bear,
> The armed rhinoceros, or th'Hyrcan tiger;
> Take any shape but that, and my firm nerves
> Shall never tremble. Or be alive again,
> And dare me to the desert with thy sword.
> If trembling I inhabit then, protest me
> The baby of a girl. Hence, horrible shadow,
> Unreal mock'ry, hence! (3.4.98–106)

The ghost calls into question any perception of a thing being what it appears to be. Moreover, the spectral presence brings the living witness closer to a state of death and a state of being less than human. The breakdown of categories here recalls those that Calpurnia inventoried in the streets of Rome. This list in *Macbeth* leaves interestingly ambiguous the nature of this "unreal mockery" that the speaker finds so horrible. Is this a phantom that mocks Macbeth or is it a mockery of his once-living friend Banquo? For the witness to the undead in this scene, it is only when the ghost "being gone, / I am a man again" (3.4.106–7). This pronouncement underscores that Macbeth can only feel human once the dead are not present.

Macbeth hopes that, with the murder of Duncan, he and his wife might "catch with his surcease, success" (1.7.3–4). Russ McDonald finds the wordplay here to be "semantically thrilling" as the phrase underscores "the aural similarity of the juxtaposed words" in a context where "neither noun is stable."[54] The "surcease," or termination, of the king or any other character brings nothing to an end because "the dead return, Banquo as a ghost, and Duncan as a corpse which needs constant tending (additional crimes) to keep it in the earth."[55] "Success," in its dual connotations of "outcome" and "following," is made complicated by the ever-blurring categories of the play. The refusal of the dead to stay buried stymies the success of Macbeth's plan and threatens to interrupt expected succession in the line of rulers.

Earlier in the play, Macbeth seemed to assuage his guilt about his deeds by thinking upon the afterlife when he wondered about "Banquo, thy soul's flight, / If it find Heaven, must find it out tonight" (3.1.142–3). The idea of heaven seems to offer solace to the surviving characters in *Macbeth.* Ross reassures himself that Macduff's family, though "fell slaughter on their souls," at least "Heaven rest them now" (4.3.229). Elsewhere in Shakespeare's work, ghosts are tied to royal succession and contribute to the burden of kings. They provide a language for thinking about past kings and about legacies. *The First Part of Henry VI* opens with the funeral of Henry V, and we find Bedford at first calling out to the departed ruler, "thy ghost I invocate: / Prosper this realm; keep it from civil broils" in hopes that the force of the ruler from beyond the grave can influence the present (1.1.52–3). Yet a few lines later, he cautions Gloucester not to inventory recent losses in front of the king's corpse lest "If Henry were recalled to life again, / These news would cause him once more yield the ghost" (1.1.66–7). Restless spirits provide a conceptual language to describe the needed king of the past and the lament about the present.[56]

We see this invocation of the afterlife as an anodyne element to justify the violence of monarchal progression again in *Richard II.* The king enjoins his comrades to "tell sad stories of the death of kings;" such storytelling involves:

> How some have been deposed, some slain in war,
> Some haunted by the ghosts they have deposed,
> Some poisoned by their wives, some sleeping killed,
> All murdered. For within the hollow crown
> That rounds the mortal temples of a king
> Keeps Death his court (3.2.152–8)

The afterlife is at the heart of the speech and at the heart of being king. Deposed kings do not depart but rather linger for the next king. Death holds court both between the "temples" (inside the mind) of the beleaguered king and in the "temples" (tombs) which will be constructed for kings when they die. When Richard says, "All murder'd," it seems he has forgotten that some kings die of natural causes. He projects the threat of his own murder onto the experiences of those in the past. Indeed, he makes clear in the play's final moments what he thinks of king-slayers when he tells his own murderer:

> Go thou, and fill another room in hell.
> *Here Exton strikes him down*
> That hand shall burn in never-quenching fire
> That staggers thus my person. Exton, thy fierce hand
> Hath with the King's blood stained the King's own land.
> (5.5.107–10)

With this set-up, Richard counterposes the fate of his murderer and the fate of his own to the destination of his soul after death. He cries, "Mount, mount, my soul; thy seat is up on high, / Whilst my gross flesh sinks downward, here to die" (5.5.111–12). And this seems to be one of the roles of the afterlife for characters in Shakespeare's plays. These individuals can imagine past deaths as presaging theirs and see ghosts—real or figurative—as apt metaphors for the ways that the past has a grip on the living.

Lady Macbeth claims that "Banquo's buried. He cannot come out on's grave" (5.1.60–1), yet the very insistence demands that we think otherwise. She, too, is troubled by the weight of the dead and realizes a closeness to the world of the supernatural. In her own efforts to fortify and "unsex" herself for the couple's murderous endeavors, Lady Macbeth calls upon "spirits / That tend on mortal thoughts" (1.5.39–40). The nature of these "spirits" is not specified, and we can variously imagine them to be either demonic entities, some physical essence deep inside of her, or her own dark thoughts. In the same speech, she invites "thick night" to come and envelop her in the "smoke of hell" in order to block the possibility that "heaven peep through the blanket of the dark / To cry 'Hold, hold!'" (1.5.52–3). At a surface level, she juxtaposes evil and good, but we also can see the afterlife at play here. Her deeds will send her to hell, in the Christian imagination certainly, and perhaps she needs to traffic with previous evil-doers to embolden herself. These "spirits" may be the ghosts of previous sinners, like those that the Porter imagines welcoming to hell. Robert N. Watson invites us to see how her "zombie-like sleepwalking mirrors Banquo's nightmarish deathwalking."[57] Her open eyes that cannot see give her the physical appearance of the dead, paralleling the death of her soul. Such an interpretation has strong resonances with Macbeth's encounter with Banquo, where the unseeing eyes of the ghost had troubled the living man's sense of himself as human.

The close proximity to the dead and the undead change Macbeth. He begins to perceive himself as neither an agent of his own will nor as a fully living being. We see this pinpointed in his famous soliloquy, which ends:

> Life's but a walking shadow, a poor player
> That struts and frets his hour upon the stage,
> And then is heard no more. It is a tale
> Told by an idiot, full of sound and fury,
> Signifying nothing. (5.5.23–7)

The use of the term "shadow" here has at least two evocative implications. On one level, humans are already dead as we have heard him use this ancient term for a ghost to describe Banquo in the banquet scene. On another level, like Plato's cave or More's vision of the afterlife as an exaggeration of earthly bliss or pain, the world occupied by the living pales in comparison to some higher plane of being and knowing. This notion that life is just an "hour upon the stage" parallels Prospero's idea of "our little life." When we acknowledge this conception of life as very brief and as a barely realized version of what it might mean to fully exist, we can think about the afterlife not as the annihilation of the self but as access to a more enduring version of the self. Carlos Eire suggests that

> we as a species have been intuiting or imagining or constructing very elaborate and sometimes elegant conceptions of *forever*, of permanence and endurance: we have imagined and even pined for whatever is the opposite of transience and impermanence and the nothingness from which we came, which always engulfs us, on all sides.[58]

If we consider our own performance in life as simply that of a woman or man playing a part (as Shakespeare often tells us), then we can imagine our earthly existence as simply a rehearsal for "the life to come" or a pantomime of some fuller experience that awaits us outside the theater of mortal existence.

4

Raising the Dead

As we have already seen, the dead re-appear with some frequency in Shakespeare's work. We might say that drama, by its nature, is an engine of resurrection. In history plays, long-dead figures find new life on the stage. In the case of tragedy, characters who died just the day before are revived for the new day's performance. In the world of the theater, actors find new life as they take on new characters. As Will West observes, "each performance unfolds already scored by previous performances, which are recalled in part by props, scripts, recordings, and other mediations, but foremost the memories of the producers of theatre, the actors, and spectators."[1] We might even extend this line of thinking to how characters in other playwrights' works function as explicit or implicit revivals of Shakespeare's characters. Beyond these instances of figurative resurrection, the dead do seem occasionally to be brought back to life in Shakespeare's work.

Necromancy, or magic involving the dead, makes evocative appearances across Shakespeare's work. In *Henry IV, Part I*, Glyndwr says he can "call spirits from the vasty deep" (3.1.51), and *The Tempest*'s Prospero says that "graves at my command / Have waked their sleepers, oped, and let 'em forth" (5.1.48–9). We will return to *The Tempest* in an extended discussion at the end of this chapter. For now, though, let us simply note that both claims can be called into question.

Necromantic Pastimes in *Henry IV, Part I*

In the case of Glyndwr's claim, we might dismiss it as an empty boast when we hear Hotspur reply, "Why, so can I, or so can any man; / But will they come when you do call for them?" (3.1.52–3). However, we find further support for the suggestion of strange relations between the Welsh and the dead when we learn that with the corpses of dead soldiers

> [...] there was such misuse,
> Such beastly shameless transformation,
> By those Welshwomen done as may not be
> Without much shame retold or spoken of. (1.1.43–6)

These depictions of relations with the dead serve political aims, as the play uses these lines to demonize the Welsh with whom Henry quarrels. The lines deploy *occupatio*, a rhetorical device where the speaker alludes to but provides no details about a tantalizing subject. The use of the term "shame" opens the possibility that the women engage in some sexually charged activity with the bodies. Holinshed's *Chronicles* (a source for many of Shakespeare's plays), describes in more detail the "shameful villainy" that the Welsh women exacted upon the English bodies, including how the women

> cut off [the corpses'] privates and put one part thereof into the mouths of every dead man, in such a sort that the cullions hung down to their chins; and not so contented, they did cut off their noses and thrust them into their tails as they lay on the ground mangled and defaced.[2]

The manner in which the dead are treated signifies the savage nature of the Welsh. Note also that the description conflates sexuality and death, suggesting ritual behaviors where the Welsh have some eldritch beliefs about relations to the dead. Joseph Roach has argued that the "necrophilic impulse [...] serves the ends of performance in a particular way" because necrophilia "seeks to preserve a sense of the relationship with the past by making physical contact with the dead."[3] In the case of *Henry IV, Part I*, the play revives English soldiers only to kill them and have them sexually abused in order to underscore the ways that political rebellions interrupt normative heterosexual reproduction. Put simply, dead soldiers cannot father children who will grow up to become more soldiers. The strange allusions to necrophilia in the aforementioned passages dramatize this by showing the uselessness of the soldiers' penises and the perverse purposes to which they are put. These English bodies stand in for the threatened demise of Englishness, and the erotic interaction with them signifies their inability to produce additional English bodies through sexual reproduction.

While the presence of a male sorcerer might strike us as unusual given the long association of witchcraft with women, an early modern audience would not interpret it as a radical departure from their sense of those who practiced magic. Of the 270 witch trials in the Elizabethan era, twenty-three of the accused were men. Well-known magicians and astrologers included John Dee (Elizabeth's court magician), Dr. Johann Faust (the German magician upon whom Marlowe's *Doctor Faustus* is based), and Simon Forman (an astrologer who moved within royal and literary circles during Shakespeare's lifetime). Playgoers would thus be familiar with male sorcerers from depictions on stage, the reputations of public figures, or conventional wisdom about learned men. In *The Golden-Grove* (1600), W. Vaughan remarks, "Nowadays among the common people, he is not adjudged any scholar at all, unless he can tell men's horoscopes, cast out devils, or hath some skill in soothsaying."[4] Vaughan's response to this common knowledge sounds much like Hotspur's: "Little do they know that this art (if it be lawful to call it an art) is the most deceitful of all arts."[5] Glyndwr, then, is a vexed figure. He at once seems to be practicing magic for which some were brought to trial while also occupying a position of power sometimes associated with men possessing occult leaning. Hotspur finds Glyndwr's boasts about black magic tedious. He reports that the sorcerer "held me last night at least nine hours / In reckoning up the several devils' names / That were his lackeys," adding "I cried, 'Hum!' and, 'Well, go to!', / But marked him not a word" (3.1.152–5). If we laugh with Hotspur's reassuring dismissal of the dark arts, we acknowledge this moment wherein "Shakespeare domesticates Glyndwr, invalidating his frightening reputation," especially combined with the later scene when "Falstaff's satirical vignette of Glyndwr mastering the force of hell (2.4.326) lays the ground for Hotspur's demystification of Glyndwr's prodigious self-image and magical pretensions."[6] Nonetheless, King Henry's description of him as "that great magician, damned Glyndwr" seems to confirm his power and his destined afterlife in hell (1.3.82).

Reunion and Resurrection in *Twelfth Night*

An expansive definition of *resurrection* helps us see this trope occurring figuratively when characters discover that someone they believed dead is in fact alive. The character in mourning may seize upon the language of the miraculous to make sense of the reunion, but these instances also remind us of the how quotidian experience prepares us for death's inevitability. Arthur Schopenhauer's notion, "Every parting gives a foretaste of death, every coming together again a foretaste of the resurrection," illuminates how we make sense of the death (and what might come after it) based on our experiences in the living world.[7] *Twelfth Night* is a play that contains no actual ghosts and features no actual resurrection. Yet it uses these terms to express the trauma of separation and the joy of reunion.

The notion of an afterlife provides comfort to those in mourning in the play. Viola states, "And what should I do in Illyria? / My brother, he is in Elysium" as a way to stress how her isolation contrasts her brother's imagined bliss in heaven (1.2.3). Viola's lament that her brother "is in Elysium" offers another instance of how references to the classical underworld intermingled with Christian visions in the early modern period. Perhaps, too, her choice of the blissful afterlife from classical literature points to her acknowledgment that this belief is in part a fiction. In the context of uncertainty about what happened to her brother after death, she simply wishes for him to be in a happy state. Olivia, too, will come to take comfort in the fact that her brother is in a pleasing afterlife. As described in the Introduction, Feste's wordplay emphasizes the foolishness of lamenting her brother's eternal state of bliss. Olivia's change in perspective about her brother's status after death assuages her grief and prepares her to transfer her loving affection first to Cesario and then to Viola's brother Sebastian.

Both Viola and Sebastian wish for a union with each other after death, mirroring characters we have seen so far who hoped to die together or to reunite in the afterlife. Sebastian opines that his father "left behind him / myself and a sister, both born in an hour," and he adds, "If the heavens / had been pleased, would we had so ended" (2.1.16–18). In his state of mourning, he attempts to maintain a closeness with her by drawing parallels between their states: "She is drowned already, sir, with salt water, though I / seem to drown her remembrance again with more" (2.1.27–8). As readers or audience members, we know that his sister survived. Here, though, his salty tears bring him some solace as he images Viola to have been lost at sea.

Viola similarly fantasizes that her body can still connect with her brother's and thereby serve as a living monument to him. Disguised as a man, she sees herself as an embodied reflection of her assumedly deceased brother:

> He named Sebastian. I my brother know
> Yet living in my glass. Even such and so
> In favour was my brother, and he went
> Still in this fashion, colour, ornament,
> For him I imitate. O, if it prove,
> Tempests are kind, and salt waves fresh in love! (3.4.371–6)

These lines suggest that Viola keeps her brother alive in her memory when she sees herself embodying the appearance of her brother. Viola takes up the metaphor of the mirror, as she becomes a copy of her brother just as the child offers a copy that continues the life of the parent. This same figurative language abounds in the Sonnets, where the speaker tells the addressee that he is his "mother's glass" and compels him to "Look in thy glass, and tell the face thou viewest / Now is the time that face should form another" (3.9, 3.1–2).[8] As Viola begins to suspect that her brother might have survived the storm, she deploys the same play of language where her salty tears might bind her to her brother lost at sea.

The reunion of the twins at the end of the play proves a scene of perceived resurrection. Still reeling from his encounters in this country where everyone seems in the grip of madness, Sebastian at first regards his sister as "drownèd Viola" (5.1.239). It seems as if he cannot make sense of her reappearance unless she is a ghost or somehow has returned from the dead. Viola, too, cannot believe that this man can be her brother because Sebastian "went he suited to his watery tomb" (5.1.232). She concludes, "If spirits can assume both form and suit / You come to fright us" (5.1.233). It is a sentiment we encountered in examples in the previous chapter, where ghosts were thought to be demons. This exchange showcases how the concept of ghosts provided a framework for understanding earthly experiences such as the lament of parting or the joy of reuniting. Indeed, in order to help his sister make sense of the strange events, Sebastian, in turn, describes himself as a ghost:

A spirit I am indeed,
But am in that dimension grossly clad
Which from the womb I did participate.
Were you a woman, as the rest goes even,
I should my tears let fall upon your cheek
And say 'Thrice-welcome, drownèd Viola'. (5.1.234–9)

Perhaps he wonders if they are both already dead, given how the strangeness of Illyria might resemble the undiscovered country of the afterlife. The close relationship between the words "Illyria" and "Elysium" might also contribute to such a confusion. On another level, this moment acknowledges how their parting constitutes a form of death and their reunion a form of resurrection. We find Shakespeare's idea that our very experience of life is an intimacy with death in Sonnet 77: "Thou by thy dial's shady stealth mayst know / Time's thievish progress to eternity" (77.7–8). Jonathan Dollimore finds these lines from the sonnet to instantiate how the sundial or clock offers "an image of death as immanent within life."[9] We can extend his claim to this unusual dialogue between Viola and Sebastian.

The mistaken identity inherent in the scene also ties to the operations of theater. Sebastian says, "Were you a woman," nodding to Orsino's own mistaking of her as a boy and the fact that the character is played by a boy actor. By calling her "drownèd Viola," he also nods to several deaths of his maiden sister in the play—in his own perception that she was lost at sea, in her assumption of the identity of Cesario, and in her forthcoming marriage to Orsino. The ending of *Twelfth Night* productively complicates Eric S. Mallin's notion that "happy endings have an atheism about them. Finality makes a *cleaner* creed than the gaping, overflowing fictions of the afterlife."[10] In addition to *Twelfth Night*, several of Shakespeare's other plays involve a realization that a character is in fact not dead. These include Helena in *All's Well That Ends Well*, Marina in *Pericles*, Hero in *Much Ado About Nothing*, and Innogen in *Cymbeline*. It is true that at the end of such plays, we do not find ourselves wondering about the present fates of such characters' souls in the afterlife. However, we should note that the notions of afterlife and resurrection provide the working vocabulary with which the characters make sense of their situation and imagine their lives after the events of the play to be happy ones.

Animating the Inanimate in *The Winter's Tale*

Another startling scene of a character's return occurs in *The Winter's Tale*, a play that leaves it ambiguous whether we are witnessing a reunion or an actual resurrection from the dead.

After the supposed death of his wife Hermione, King Leontes does not remarry because doing so "would make her sainted spirit / Again possess her corpse, and on this stage, / Where we offenders mourn, appear soul-vexed" (5.1.57–9). In his imagination, remaining a widower keeps Hermione resting in her tomb peacefully. In terms of the needs of the narrative, his fear of waking the dead also obviates complications by ensuring that he is available to her when she will seemingly return from the grave. The notion that she is "sainted" suggests a purification of her soul upon death, if even only in the sense that he now realizes the foolishness of his concern that she had been unfaithful. The depiction of the deceased wife as saintly parallels John Milton's later poem in which he recounts reuniting with his dead wife in a dream. "Methought I Saw My Late Espoused Saint" explicitly refers to the myth of Alcestis, a story to which we will see Shakespeare nods as well.

Paulina, the queen's friend, imagines how she would behave were she Hermione's ghost in the event that Leontes had re-married:

> Were I the ghost that walked I'd bid you mark
> Her eye, and tell me for what dull part in't
> You chose her. Then I'd shriek that even your ears
> Should rift to hear me, and the words that followed
> Should be, "Remember mine". (5.1.63–7)

In Paulina's depiction, we hear echoes of other ghosts in Shakespeare. The imagined spirit would have vengeful leanings and would demand to be remembered in the event of the spouse re-marrying. In this, we can find strong parallels to King Hamlet. In fact, Frances Dolan posits that "although there is not a ghostly mother in Shakespeare's plays to rival Hamlet's father, *The Winter's Tale* comes closest to imagining an undead mother."[11] Certainly, the final mandate here ("Remember mine") strongly recalls King Hamlet's "Remember me."

At end of the play, Leontes' love and contrition seem to bring his wife Hermione back from the dead. After an extended period of mourning, Pauline presents Leontes with a deeply lifelike statue of the queen. Just as Hermione is rendered a "saint" when her husband realized how he wronged her in retrospect after her seeming death, Leontes will undergo a purifying experience as he witnesses her resurrection. As Sarah Beckwith puts it, "Leontes is transformed in his understanding of himself—sinful and redeemed from sin in one and the same moment, as the past is carried into a redeemed memory."[12] The final scene of the play thus dramatizes Judith Butler's notion that overcoming mourning does not simply involve transferring our affections to a new beloved object (as Freud suggests), but rather undergoing a profound change within ourselves.

After revealing the statue of the late wife, Paulina announces, "Music, awake her; strike!" After music plays, she continues:

> 'Tis time. Descend. Be stone no more. Approach.
> Strike all that look upon with marvel. Come,
> I'll fill your grave up. Stir. Nay, come away.
> Bequeath to death your numbness, for from him
> Dear life redeems you.
> (*To Leontes*) You perceive she stirs. (5.3.98–103)

This rich passage contributes to the ambiguity of this scene of resurrection while also calling our attention to how powerful the language of unexpected reunion can be. The reference to a "grave" leaves ambiguous whether Hermione actually had been dead and buried, or if some elaborate ruse involved an empty grave. The possibility of two Hermiones, one in the grave and one inhabiting an afterlife now on stage, invokes the notion of *et in arcadia ego*, the famous inscription on the shepherd's tomb in the painting described earlier in Chapter 2. The use of "bequeath" invokes the language of wills and implies that this will be a second life. As we will see next, the scene is multivalent in terms of how it invokes several ancient myths. After Hermione descends from the pedestal, Paulina warns:

> Start not. Her actions shall be holy as
> You hear my spell is lawful. Do not shun her
> Until you see her die again, for then
> You kill her double. Nay, present your hand.
> When she was young, you wooed her. Now, in age,
> Is she become the suitor? (5.3.104–9)

Resurrection gives new power as she becomes the "suitor" and he becomes the contrite lover presenting himself in hopes of her acceptance. However, this entity should not frighten him, and he should woo her. Leontes is stunned, "O, she's warm! / If this be magic, let it be an art / Lawful as eating" (5.3.109–11). The repetition of "lawful" across Paulina's description and Leontes' response underscores that this magic should be interpreted as good or "holy." We see a play on "art" here as it describes both nature and the artist's creative process. This is not the necromantic meddling with dead bodies that made Glyndwr such a troubling (or perhaps laughable) character in *Henry IV, Part I.* Rather, this seeming miracle brings about a happy ending and showcases the theater as a space for resurrection.

This scene would remind playgoers of several myths from classical antiquity. A statue that comes to life might register as a nod to the story of the sculptor Pygmalion, whose desire for a lover is fulfilled when Venus brings his creation to life. However, Hermione is not simply a stone statue transformed into a person; she is a human being brought back from the dead. Thus we also see invoked those ancient figures reclaimed from Hades' clutch. For example, Hercules rescues Theseus (but not Theseus' beloved friend Pirithous) from the underworld, and in another instance, he rescues Alcestis and returns her to her loving husband Admetus. When Hermione returns from the dead, Paulina will warn "it appears she lives, / Though yet she speak not" (5.3.118–19). This idea that she will not speak parallels the state of Alcestis when first retrieved by Hercules. Early modern playgoers might also recognize in *The Winter's Tale* the story of Orpheus' failed attempt to save Eurydice from the clutches of the king of the underworld. Indeed, Colin Burrow notes that "Orpheus, the singer of Ovid's tale of Pygmalion, is also a background presence in this tale about a man hoping to see his wife return to life through art, since Orpheus of course went to the underworld in a vain attempt to rescue his wife from death."[13] Certainly, the phrase "music stirs here" cannot help but remind some playgoers of the magic of Orpheus.

Yet another myth becomes visible in this play when Hermione and Leontes' daughter, Perdita, invoke the name of an ancient figure who was kidnapped by Hades and forced to dwell in the underworld: "O Proserpina, / For the flowers now that, frighted, thou letst fall / From Dis's wagon!" (4.4.116–18). The mythical Proserpina returned for six months each year to join her mother, the goddess of agriculture, during spring and summer. The ancient story thus intermingles a variety of themes that we can trace in *The Winter's Tale*: mourning, separation, cyclicality, and the return of the dead to reunite the family. In fact, Marjorie B. Garber suggests that the tale of Proserpina "is the one Ovidian myth that—beyond all others—informs the play."[14] The title itself pinpoints how the narrative will draw power from the notion of *returning* as the symbolic language of seasons emphasizes the coming of life after seeming death in the botanical world. Leontes' friend Polixenes witnesses the reanimated Hermione and exclaims, "how stol'n from the dead" (5.3.116). The use of "stol'n" reminds us of how unnatural it is for humans to move in reverse, to recover from death. The choice of term also underscores the value of life, the preciousness of one soul brought back into the world of the living. "Stol'n" also foregrounds the crucial role of the person doing the resurrecting—Hercules, Orpheus, Paulina, and the author himself—in bringing the dead to life.[15]

Resurrecting Medea in *The Tempest*

Toward the end of *The Tempest*, Prospero delivers a speech in which he claims capabilities as-yet unseen in the narrative—including reviving the dead (5.1.42–60). The speech draws directly from an incantation by the sorceress Medea in Book 7 of Ovid's *Metamorphoses.* In fact, Shakespeare changes the wording only slightly from Arthur Golding's 1567 English translation of Ovid's epic. The resuscitation of Medea evocatively transports the language not only across time but also across genders and narratives. Prospero himself seems to embrace the earlier text as a means by which to express his power and, in doing so, reflects Shakespeare's own authorial process. As the contemporary of Shakespeare, Frances Meres, famously says of him: "[. . .] the sweet witty soul of *Ovid* lives in mellifluous & honey-tongued *Shakespeare.*"[16] Amidst Prospero's claims to resurrect the dead, Shakespeare resurrects an ancient poet and his sorceress.

Prospero asserts here that he has raised the dead, although we do not necessarily see him do so in the play. It is possible that he describes events prior to the play or that he uses the notion of resurrection metaphorically. Prospero's speech does make a series of claims to unwitnessed mystical power that can be variously explained by events in the play. His claim to "have bedimmed / The noontide sun" could describe the storm that Ariel has caused at his master's command or could meta-theatrically describe Shakespeare's ability to have his audience imagine nighttime while at the theater during the day (5.1.41–2). His claim to have "called forth the mutinous winds, / And 'twixt the green sea and the azured vault / Set roaring war" could similarly track to the tempest that incites the action of the play (5.1.42–4). And while the lines that follow might also describe the storm that wrecks the boat, the lines equally could describe Prospero's freeing of Ariel from his prison in a tree:

> [. . .] to the dread rattling thunder
> Have I given fire, and rifted Jove's stout oak
> With his own bolt; the strong-based promontory
> Have I made shake, and by the spurs plucked up
> The pine and cedar (5.1.44–8)

It is the speech's final claim, however, that is the most striking and might give us the most pause: "graves at my command / Have waked their sleepers, oped, and let 'em forth / By my so potent art" (5.1.48–50). It is the only claim that cannot be located easily in the narrative. On one level, we might interpret Prospero's allusion to resurrection as meta-theatrical: he ends the highly orchestrated events on the island by gathering characters who have assumed that each other has drowned. On another level, his speech revivifies dead voices: those of Ovid and his character Medea. Because Prospero will renounce his powers shortly after this speech, Sean Benson suggests that "having resurrected the dead, Prospero had apparently unleashed a kind of nightmarish world."[17] An alternate reading of the text would be that Prospero revives Ovid here to bring harmony between the characters and between literary traditions.

In Shakespeare's source text, Medea does in fact bring the dead to life. Arthur Golding's version of the speech reads:

> You airs and wind: you elves of hills, of brooks, of woods alone,
> Of standing lakes, and of the night approach you everyone.
> Through help of whom (the crooked banks much wondering at
>   the thing)
> I have compelled streams to run clean backward to their spring.

By charms I make the calm seas rough, and make the rough seas
 plain,
And cover all the sky with clouds and chase them thence again.
By charms, I raise and lay the winds and burst the viper's jaw.
And from the bowels of the earth both stones and trees do draw.
Whole woods and forests I remove. I make the mountains shake,
And even the earth itself to groan and fearfully to quake.
I call up dead men from their graves, and thee lightsome moon
I darken often, though beaten brass abate thy peril soon.
Our sorcery dims the morning fair and darkens the sun at noon.
(7.188–200)[18]

Shakespeare does not use the speech word-for-word, but most of his changes might be attributed to regularizing the language into iambic pentameter or omitting some specific plot points from the older story. Interestingly, he omits the line "I have compelled streams to run clean backward to their spring." Perhaps it would seem too overt a reference to the play's use of an older text. The line's omission urges us to explore a nuanced explanatory model for understanding Shakespeare's use of Ovid in *The Tempest*, and the notions of the afterlife and the resurrection of the dead provide such a model.

When we take as our focus how Prospero's speech appropriates words spoken by Medea, we find ourselves meditating on the absent, the missing, the unacknowledged. Although a scene of physical resurrection is not here in the play, the narrative brims with spectral stories and with phantom figures. Haunting Prospero's speech is the figure of Medea, who does indeed revivify her lover Jason's father, Aeson. Her story is muted as it is subsumed into Prospero's story, and we could align this elision with the larger absence of female characters, aside from Prospero's daughter, in the play. Melissa Sanchez has argued that Miranda is accompanied by "ghostly surrogates"—including Sycorax (the witch who sired Caliban), Claribel (the daughter of the King of Naples), and Dido (who is mentioned in passing in a conversation between Gonzalo, Antonio, and Sebastian). We could add Medea to the list of spectral female figures that haunt the play, especially because Sanchez adds that "the erotic dimension these figures bring to the play disrupts simple narratives of dominance, submission, and revolt."[19] In the main action of the play, Miranda becomes subjected to patriarchal rule through her marriage to Ferdinand. Still the play's explicit allusion to Dido and implicit allusion to Medea remind us that this marriage may yet fail and that women can prove more powerful than men, particularly given that the ancient sorceress actually has done something Prospero may exaggerate his ability to do.[20]

The Tempest is not the only place in Shakespeare where Medea casts a shadow over marriages. The most prominent example is *The Merchant of Venice*, where Shakespeare makes several overt allusions to the story of Jason and Medea. Jessica likens her nighttime elopement with Lorenzo to "such a night / Medea gatherèd the enchanted herbs / That did renew old Aeson" (5.1.12–14). The comparison is not necessarily positive, as the conversation also invokes the figures of Cressida, Dido, and Thisbe (5.1.6–10). Thus, on some level, the comparison to Medea falls in line with the others to suggest that Lorenzo eventually will leave her, despite sacrifices she might make for him. At the same time, the reference to resurrection of Aeson suggests Jessica's own rebirth, in turn inviting us to consider Medea as a figure who stands for second chances. If Medea can revive old Aeson and give him a second chance at life, perhaps Jessica and Lorenzo might have a different outcome than that of Medea and Jason.[21] Portia, too, is connected to Medea. Bassanio describes her this way:

> [. . .] her sunny locks
> Hang on her temples like a golden fleece,
> Which makes her seat of Belmont Colchis' strand,
> And many Jasons come in quest of her. (1.1.169–72)

The connection is concretized when Gratiano proclaims, "We are the Jasons; we have won the fleece," once the marriages to Portia and Nerissa are secured (3.2.239). There are now multiple Jasons, underscoring that the story from Ovid is multivalent for Shakespeare. Portia represents both the fleece and Medea, she surely resurrects Antonio from a death sentence and perhaps resurrects Shylock, too, when he is forcedly reborn a Christian.

Whereas the suitors in *The Merchant of Venice* find their Medea in Portia and Lorenzo finds his in Jessica, *The Tempest*'s sailors and lovers encounter a more spectral Medea in Prospero's power and in his words. Might we say, then, that this later play without many women is a play about missing women? Miranda does not remember her mother, though she does recall a group of women who attended to her. Sycorax died before Prospero arrived. The possibility that Ariel might be female—adduced when he takes the form of a harpy and when Prospero's refers to him as "My Ariel, chick"—is foreclosed (5.1.320). Ovid's Medea is an unnamed voice at the climax of the play. She is subsumed into Prospero's speech, just as Ovid's own play entitled *Medea* (his only known work of drama) has been lost to us.

Prospero's speech is not entirely lifted from Ovid. He includes a detail found neither in Golding's translation nor in Ovid's original. He describes the "printless foot" of the "elves" and "demi-puppets" who he curiously addresses in this scene (5.1.34–6). Might he draw upon the commonplace of referring to the work of previous authors in terms of poetic footsteps? The phrase recalls Sir Philip Sidney's complaint that "others' feet still seemed but strangers in my way" when Astrophil attempts to woo his Stella.[22] Barbara Mowat notes that we never actually see Prospero's book and subsequently posits that "Prospero himself is simultaneously [...] a serious master of spirits and a stage-or-romance wizard who also reminds us [...] of a Renaissance magus and a Jacobean street magician."[23] The notion of Prospero as a stage or street performer recently found expression in a production of the play directed by the Las Vegas magician Teller (of Penn and Teller fame) which features a number of old school tricks. The sleight of hand to which Mowat alludes helps us to imagine the speech as a feat of *sprezzatura*. That is, Prospero draws upon his learned study to produce this short speech, re-articulating words written by an earlier writer, as one might do in courtly performance. Prospero thereby fashions himself through his capacity to remember others' words. This can be linked to the larger thrust of the play's plot, which revolves around the magician's memory of what was done to him and his need to reckon with the memory in the present. The strong connections between the past and the present in *The Tempest* lead Sarah Beckwith to claim that "Prospero's project of restitution [...] is utterly tied up with the question of recall and memory."[24] An exploration of the resurrected figure of Medea in this play illuminates how Prospero wrestles with both his own personal memories and larger cultural memories that inform the early modern period.

Stephen Orgel interprets the adopted speech from Medea to signal that Prospero's "most potent art" is "revealed as translation and interpretation" as the ancient sorceress first becomes incorporated into the figure of Sycorax and then is shown to be an aspect of Prospero himself.[25] This magician's performance is not just translation, though. More specifically, it is an instance of *translatio studii et imperii*, the popular early modern notion that "with the knowledge, comes the power." That is, the translation of ancient texts could bring with it the power that made possible the accomplishments of the ancient empires of Greece and Rome. *The Tempest* dramatizes this concept because Prospero's very command of a classical voice links to his power.

Both Prospero's and Medea's speeches concede that their sorcerous powers derive, at least in part, from others. Like Medea, Prospero credits the "elves" for their help with his magic, and this reference to helpers in *The Tempest* may very well refer to Ariel and his "meaner ministers" who have performed bits of magic throughout the play and specifically at the masque at Miranda and Ferdinand's wedding. It seems that Prospero's way is to put everyone to work. This is hardly the utopia envisioned by Gonzalo, when the aging courtier is asked how he'd envision the perfect island society. He depicts a community with "use of service, none" and "no occupation, all men idle, all" (2.1.157, 2.1.160). In Prospero's utopia, everyone is working. That is, everyone but him and Miranda. And these workers in the play have connections to tropes of resurrection. The ways in which Prospero displays mastery over the island, the labors of everyone on it, and even the words of others that enable such control underlines how much of this power derives from co-opting the efforts of others. Shakespeare and Prospero perform ownership over the words and characters of previous authors by way of scant citation. Because they do not overtly name their sources, they implicitly assert that authority to call the power of past figures their own.

The logics wherein Medea's capabilities might be transferred to another person are already built into Ovid's tale. Her magic can not only achieve wondrous feats but also allow others to accomplish marvels. Jason overcomes challenges on Colchos because of enchanted herbs that she prepares for him. Her spell-making empowers herbs, and these become the means by which she transfers power to Jason: "she believed; and straight he received the magic herbs and learned their use, then withdrew full of job into his lodging" (7.98–9).[26] Indeed, Jason's use of Medea's herbs allows him to perform a range of feats that link him to Prospero, including control of the elements and the ability to induce sleep:

> After Jason had sprinkled upon him the Lethaean juice of a certain herb and thrice had recited the words that bring peaceful slumber, which stay the swollen sea and swift-flowing rivers, then sleep came to those eyes which had never known sleep before, and the heroic son of Aeson gained the golden fleece. (7.152–6)

These track to supernatural acts that Prospero by himself and with the help of others has accomplished: putting Miranda to sleep and commanding the sea. Indeed, Miranda asks her father if it is by "your art" that the weather changes so quickly, and the phrase echoes Prospero's phrase, "my art" moments later, a phrase which in turn echoes Medea's "my art" just before she performs the resurrection of Aeson (1.2.1, 1.2.25, 7.176). It is only sixty lines after the resurrection that Medea will begin the speech that Prospero ventriloquizes, a speech which articulates her claims to command rivers and seas. Here the *Metamorphoses* models how Medea's power might be co-opted by men, where Jason obtains them through herbs. In *The Tempest*, Shakespeare's and Prospero's *magic* involves bringing old texts back to life in early modern contexts.

The use of writing from an older author such as Ovid and dialogue from an older figure such as Medea reminds us that all writing is, to some extent, *ghost-written* by entities from the past who inhabit the writer's mind. As Barthes puts so nicely, "language is for [the writer] a frontier, to overstep which alone might lead to the linguistically supernatural; it is a field of action, the definition of, and hope for, a possibility."[27] While for Barthes' thoroughly modern sensibilities "under the name of style a self-sufficient language is evolved which has its roots only in the depths of the author's personal and secret mythology,"[28] Shakespeare operates in the context of authorship desiring not to break from the past. As M. L. Stapleton observes, "just as Ovid before Shakespeare knew that the jerks of invention are simply impossible without predecessors to refashion and reanimate."[29] Differentiation is not necessarily the goal of early modern writers, who so often seek to revivify dead voices within their own. Indeed, Barthes invokes Orpheus' looking back to confirm Eurydice trailing during the ascent from the underworld as a signal of what the author consciously avoids.

This would strike Shakespeare as alien both because the mythological figure constituted the paradigmatic poet for Renaissance readers and because the Renaissance writer makes her or his retrospection so evident.

Shakespeare condenses and regularizes the meter that he inherits from Ovid and Golding. In some instances, the playwright's re-workings cause Prospero's magic to appear much more aggressive than Medea's. While Prospero has "twixt the green sea and azured vault / set roaring war," Medea tells us that she can "make the calm seas rough, and make the rough seas plain." Prospero has "call'd forth the mutinous winds." Yet Medea might "cover all the sky with clouds," but she also will "chase them thence again"; she will "raise *and* lay the winds" (my emphasis). Medea uses her power to maintain balance, it would seem, rather than to enforce her will continually on others. Her claim to raising the dead follows these lines almost immediately, suggesting that these resurrections are meant to balance some other force in the world. Such a reading finds support in her choice to return to a balanced pair at the end of the speech:

> I call up dead men from their graves: and thee lightsome moon
> I darken oft, though beaten brass abate thy peril soon.
> Our sorcery dims the morning faire, and darkens the sun at noon.

In light of the context of Medea's claim about raising the dead (both that the act appears alongside depictions of quelling the weather and that the act is an expression of love for Jason), I believe that it goes too far to suggest, as one scholar does, that Prospero "recoils from the thought of what he has done, recalling such resurrections with the same horror as did Medea."[30] Prospero's speech mixes assertions about things he has and has not done, while Medea's speech strikes me as one tinged with themes of reconciliation rather than horror. Tracing lines of textual resurrection in the play helps us see why Katherine Heavey asserts that Prospero is "doubly Medea-like, echoing her words and, through his cruelty to Ariel, inadvertently revealing his similarity to the Medea-like Sycorax."[31] When we consider Prospero's place in literary history, we may find ourselves re-considering our opinion as to whether he is the hero or villain of this play.

The phantom presence of Medea in *The Tempest* finds intriguing expression in Julie Taymor's decision to re-imagine Prospero as a

Figure 4.1. Helen Mirren as Prospera, as Taymor channels both Shakespeare and Medea. *The Tempest* (Dir. Taymor, Miramax, 2010).

female "Prospera" in the director's recent film version titled *The Tempest*.[32] The seamlessness with which the gender switch takes place can be credited partially to Helen Mirren's magisterial acting, but the ease of the shift also owes itself to Shakespeare's use of Ovid (Figure 4.1).

Taymor cites her own realization that a crucial speech was originally spoken by Medea as contributing to her realization that the character could be played by a woman.[33] So inspired, Taymor makes several decisions regarding her film. For example, Prospera is expelled from Milan not only because of her brother's zeal for power but also because of rumors he spreads about her having killed her husband. To drive home the linkages between Prospero's sorcery and witchcraft, Taymor interpolates into the script the line "knowing that others of my sex have burned for far less." As Medea changes to Prospero in Shakespeare's play and Prospero to Prospera in Taymor's film, one cannot help but sense the Ovidian-ness of the whole enterprise. As Lisa S. Starks-Estes notes regarding the use of Ovid by Renaissance writers, "this method of one tale morphing into the next [...] is based on the poetics of transformation they saw in Ovid's *Metamorphoses*."[34] The playwright absorbs and voices Ovid, just as Prospero does Medea.

These many layers of voices and of figures take us back to the unseen object at the center of the play: Prospero's book(s). While Caliban refers to his master having "books" in the plural, Prospero suggests he only has one book when he promises to relinquish his power. He announces,

> But this rough magic
> I here abjure. And when I have required
> Some heavenly music—which even now I do—
> To work mine end upon their senses that
> This airy charm is for, I'll break my staff,
> Bury it certain fathoms in the earth,
> And deeper than did ever plummet sound
> I'll drown my book. (5.1.50–7)

The notion that Prospero's book might be a commonplace book could explain why he uses the singular here. It also suggests that what he will "abjure" will be the courtly practice of quoting others. If he plans to drown a book that he has written in (rather than ones he has read), this statement at the end of the play—"I'll drown my book"—foretells a rejection of not just the dark arts, but of his past and of his memory.

Even if we set aside for a moment the interpretation that his drowned book could be a commonplace journal, the possibilities for how to imagine the nature of Prospero's absent book(s) remain tantalizing. Peter Greenaway's film adaptation helps us consider that the books might be volumes of Ovid's *Metamorphoses.*[35] In *Prospero's Books*, the texts available to the magician include a series of titles that could refer to Ovid's works: *A Book of Mythologies*, *An Atlas Belonging to Orpheus*, *The Ninety-Two Conceits of the Minotaur*, *A Book of Love*, *The Autobiographies of Pasiphae and Semiramis.* In Greenaway's film, John Gielgud's Prospero is both a reader of these books and a writer of books, as we see him actively scripting the dialogue of the other characters. Gielgud also voices the lines of other characters, depicting the kind of polyvocality at work in Prospero's words that we know to be Medea's and widely imagine to be Shakespeare's own farewell to the theater. Greenaway's presentation of *The Tempest* on screen offers a resurrection of the original play where we cannot disaggregate readings and voices. Such an approach urges us to avoid looking for straight lines of genealogy or for single points of origin that clearly map earlier texts to later texts. In other words, we can embrace the idea that adaptations by nature resurrect previous texts and, even if aspiring toward utmost fidelity, will still alter the previous text by placing it in a new context.

Prospero's appropriation of Medea's speech in *The Tempest* reminds us of just how evocative resurrection can be. His claims to have necromantically raised the dead provide evidence for the darker implications of his magic while also pointing us toward the important role of the *presence of absence* in the play. Taymor and Greenaway emphasize that Prospero's voice inevitably constitutes multiple voices and that the figure of Medea in the text, like that of Prospero's book(s), might best serve us if it remains evocatively unlocatable. It is the absence of these voices and this figure that allows us to consider the complexities involved when earlier writers surface in later texts. Such instances offer opportunities to consider how the vitality of Shakespeare's art relied upon bringing earlier writers back to life and how the continued vitality of his work in the present is fueled by generating new interpretations of its place in literary history.

5

Achieving Immortality

We can understand the term *afterlife* to denote not just what will happen to us after our own earthly lives are complete, but also what will happen in the living world as it progresses without us. That is, what *after-effects* will our lives have once we are gone?

In his recent philosophical ruminations on the subject, Samuel Scheffler suggests that our contemporary culture now largely conceives of the afterlife in secular terms because we live in an era when so many people believe that life ends at the biological termination of the body. In Scheffler's view, humans grappling with mortality are deeply concerned with what will occur on Earth after they die. He puts it this way, "what happens after our deaths matters to us in its own right and, in addition, our confidence that there will be an afterlife is a condition of many of the things mattering to us here and now."[1] According to Scheffler, we are invested *both* in there simply being a future *and* in the notion that we can shape that future. While he sees this as a particularly contemporary and largely atheistic perspective on death, such a sentiment also circulated in the early modern period. Keith Thomas suggests that personal fame in the living world offered a compelling strategy for early moderns to continue living in the physical world after death. The early modern obsession with everlasting reputation was "so much so," he writes "as to make one doubt whether the Christian doctrine of the afterlife can have been a living reality for those to whom posthumous fame was so overriding an objective."[2] We can hear resonances of both Scheffler's and Thomas' claims in Richard Crompton's *The Mansion of Magnanimity* (1599), which positions reputation and fame as means to secure a posthumous afterlife among the living. Crompton advises, "every man that desires to live in name when he is dead ought to endeavour himself to leave some memory of his virtues or worthy acts."[3] The phrases "live in name when he is dead" and "leave some memory" imply more than just dying with the hope that others occasionally will remember you. Instead, they suggest that one can take an active stance while alive and bequeath something to the world that will secure a conceivable form of immortality.

The idea that one should "leave some memory" certainly echoes language in Shakespeare's plays and sonnets that urge adults to have children. Viola admonishes Olivia for letting her beauty go to waste such that she would "leave the world no copy" if she dies childless (1.5.232). Similarly, the speaker of the sonnets urges the young man to have a child because "His tender heir might bear his memory" (1.4). Variations of the word "leave" appear eighteen times across the sonnets. The term is used variously throughout the poems, possessing different meanings in different contexts and also carrying multiple meanings in single instances. At times, the term refers to the addressee leaving the world, and particularly leaving the speaker. In other cases, it refers to leaves on trees that offer figurative language with which to depict the inevitability of aging and the passing of time. "Leave" in the sonnets thus serves the specific project of urging the addressee to have a child and the broader project of describing the experience of loss. At the same time, the term points to the paper pages upon which these poems have been printed.

Due in part to the affordability of print and the expanding book trade in the early modern period, writing offered the appealing promise of continuing a person's presence after death, and thus ensuring a form of immortality. In 1581, the translator George Pettie wrote that "The only way to win mortality is either to do things worth the writing, or to write the things worth the reading."[4] We certainly see this in the dual purpose of Shakespeare's sonnets. The speaker explicitly highlights the poems as objects that will immortalize the aging addressee, all the while implicitly emphasizing that Shakespeare's immortality will be secured by the publishing of the poems. Shakespeare was not alone in realizing that literature was a path to a foreseeable afterlife. One of his contemporaries, Thomas Nashe, remarks that "There is no immorality given a man on earth like unto plays."[5]

The notion that personal fame constitutes a vital form of afterlife is one that we can trace back to antiquity. The ancient Greeks and

Romans believed that the afterlife was a gray and joyless location, where the dead retained no memory of their former lives. This placed increased pressure, then, upon the living to create lasting reputations. The figure of Achilles offers a useful case study for this line of thinking. In a famous instance from Homer's *Iliad*, Achilles' mother comes to him and delivers a prophecy. She informs him that he has a choice. He can fight in the Trojan War and, in doing so, die but subsequently achieve everlasting fame. Or he can go home, live to an old age, and be forgotten by generations to come. He chooses to go to war. In another important instance, Plato's *Symposium* describes fame as a form of immortal offspring that is equal to or superior to human children. While Christian visions of supernatural afterlives characterized by bliss or torment for the soul superseded ancient visions of a banal underworld, this notion that a continued presence in cultural memory constituted a viable form of immortality seems to have subsisted well into the early modern period and beyond.

Shakespeare's Afterlife in Folio (and Beyond)

In the discussion of early modern tombs, we saw how physical structures served to keep the dead alive in the minds of the living, especially as individuals seemed to speak from the afterlife in order to pass along some wisdom to those who happened upon their grave markers. Epitaphs do not solely appear on tombstones, however. As short poems that honor the dead, epitaphs appear in printed books and in performance (as we saw in the case of *Timon of Athens*, mentioned earlier). Indeed, poems of mourning have a prominent place in the early editions of Shakespeare's collected work. And while these epitaphs appear in his printed works rather than on his tombstone, they position his works as monuments to his life and as testimonies to his immortality.[6]

In the 1623 *Comedies, Histories, and Tragedies* (often referred to as the "First Folio"), Hugh Holland's sonnet "Upon the Lines and Life of the Famous Scenic Poet, Master William Shakespeare" ends with the couplet, "For though his line of life went soon about, / The life yet of his lines shall never out" (13–14). The poem disaggregates Shakespeare from his work, suggesting that the author's physical body will die but his writing will take on some qualities of a living being and continue thriving in the world. We might also note that "lines" not only functions as metonymy for the playwright's larger body of work, but also likens his texts to the genealogical lines of children. Leonard Digges' "To the memory of the deceased author Master William Shakespeare" relates how the deceased playwright's works will outlive his physical tomb:

> And time dissolves thy Stratford monument,
> Here we alive shall view thee still. This book,
> When brass and marble fade, shall make thee look
> Fresh to all ages. (4–7)

The language here recalls Sonnet 55 and Sonnet 107 that depict brass and marble, respectively, as unable to outlive Shakespeare's verse (55.1, 107.14). Digges' closing lines, "our Shakespeare, thou canst never die, / But crowned with laurel, live eternally" places the responsibility upon the living ("our") to keep the deceased alive (21–2). Ben Jonson also contributes a poem to the First Folio, writing "Thou art a monument without a tomb, / And art alive still while thy book doth live / And we have wits to read and praise to give" (22–4). The idea that future readers guarantee Shakespeare's continued life mirrors Digges' logic and adds that the playwright needs no grave marker. Indeed, Jonson seems to combine the ideas in Holland's and Digges' poems: the playwright is not dead, as his works have taken on a lifelike appearance of the writer himself. It is almost as if Shakespeare exists outside the constraints of normative temporality. Jonson's famous claim, "He was not of an age, but for all time," seems to suggest as much as it ties the timelessness of Shakespeare's work to personal immortality (44).

In the 1632 *Comedies, Histories, and Tragedies* (often referred to as the "Second Folio"), additional dedicatory verse builds upon the themes of the commendatory poems included in the First Folio. An author simply identified as "I.M.S." frames the act of reading the included plays as a form of resurrection because "Shakespeare shall breath and speak" within the volume's pages (73). James Mabbe similarly highlights the book as a vessel through which the author returns to the theater of life: "We thought thee dead, but this thy printed worth / Tells thy spectators that thou went'st but forth / to enter with applause" (3–5). In Mabbe's formulation, the Second Folio can be construed as an encore for this star. Each new publication of Shakespeare's work is a new appearance of the beloved actor, who only appeared to conclude his career performance with his physical death. John Milton contributes an unattributed poetic epitaph for Shakespeare, and it represents the young poet's first published work. Milton's "An Epitaph on the Admirable Dramatic Poet, William Shakespeare" echoes some of the ideas expressed by writers in the First Folio, quoted here earlier, while adding an important distinction (Figure 1.1). He suggests that Shakespeare's "honoured bones" need no "pilèd stones," emphasizing that literary works themselves can function as monuments to the dead (1–2). He further underlines the importance of readers in keeping dead writers alive as "our wonder and astonishment" function as the absent physical "monument" (7–8). Milton's Shakespeare, too, seems positioned outside of time.

The playwright's lines are "Delphic," making such a deep impression because they speak to future events and affect future audiences (12). In the collection titled *Poems*, eight years after the Second Folio, dedicatory writers continue the trend of praising Shakespeare and insisting on his immortality. For example, John Warren finds Shakespeare "again revived," "twice lived," and "immortal" in his commendatory poem in the same volume (1, 2, 6).

As these writers praise Shakespeare and testify to his immortality, they are of course attempting to secure their own afterlives in the imaginations of readers. However, most of these writers of the commendatory verse will be unknown to today's readers. Intriguingly, Milton, who appears anonymously in the Second Folio, arguably now rivals Shakespeare for the position of the finest writer in English. In the 1640 *Poems,* Leonard Digges makes overt his desire to become someone who would possess Milton's cultural stature today. He asks the question, "why do I dead Shakespeare's praise recite?"; then he immediately answers, "Some second Shakespeare must of Shakespeare write" (65–6). Digges' verses appeared posthumously in the *Poems,* suggesting that although he did not become the "second Shakespeare," he did experience a sort of revival in his published verse.

The fantasy that Shakespeare could be revived by the publication and performance of his work finds curious expression in instances of Shakespeare's ghost appearing in narratives or on stage.[7] Shakespeare appears as a ghost for the first time in the prologue to John Dryden's

Vpon the Effigies of my worthy Friend, the Author Mafter VVilliam Shakefpeare, and his VVorkes.

Spectator, this Lifes Shaddow is; To fee
The truer image and a livelier he
Turne Reader. But, obferve his Comicke vaine,
Laugh, and proceed next to a Tragicke ftraine,
Then weepe; So when thou find'ft two contraries,
Two different paffions from thy rapt foule rife,
Say, (who alone effect fuch wonders could)
Rare Shake-fpeare *to the life thou doft behold.*

An Epitaph on the admirable Dramaticke Poet, VV.SHAKESPEARE.

What neede my Shakefpeare *for his honour'd bones,*
The labour of an Age, in piled ftones
Or that his hallow'd Reliques fhould be hid
Vnder a ftarre-ypointing Pyramid?
Deare Sonne of Memory, great Heire of Fame,
What needft thou fuch dull witneffe of thy Name?
Thou in our wonder and aftonifhment
Haft built thy felfe a lafting Monument:
For whil'ft to th'fhame of flow-endevouring Art
Thy eafie numbers flow, and that each part,
Hath from the leaves of thy unvalued Booke,
Thofe Delphicke Lines with deepe Impreffion tooke
Then thou our fancy of her felfe bereaving,
Doft make us Marble with too much conceiving,
And fo Sepulcher'd in fuch pompe doft lie
That Kings for fuch a Tombe would wifh to die.

Figure 5.1. Two commendatory poems in the Second Folio. The second one was penned by John Milton. *Mr. William Shakespeare's Comedies, Histories, and Tragedies.*

Troilus and Cressida (1679), where he testifies to the faithfulness of the adaptation. He also appears in the anonymous *The Visitation, Or An Interview between the Ghost of Shakespeare and D-v-d G-rr–k, Esq.* (1755), where the playwright returns from the dead to admonish the actor for not performing the plays with sufficient authenticity and adherence to their intended mode. Should we be surprised? To this day, audience members disagree whether certain Shakespearean adaptations take too much liberty with the original text or represent vital ways to keep the original stories alive. To resurrect Shakespeare on stage, screen, or page assumes the notion that we could somehow know the author's original intent. Perhaps writers continually resurrect Shakespeare because we feel he did not receive a proper send-off at the time of his death. Indeed, Marjorie B. Garber even frames Lawrence Olivier's burial in Westminster Abbey as "through a mechanism of displacement, the memorial service for Olivier becomes a memorial service for Shakespeare."[8] The ways in which props from plays and photos of the costumed actor were used in obituaries engendered "a state funeral for the poet playwright who defines western culture, doing him appropriate homage."[9] Indeed, Paul Franssen's study of representations of Shakespeare as a character in depictions from the seventeenth century to the present finds them to be "an index to the ways in which we use cultural icons to make sense of our lives, our ideals and fears, as individuals or collectively."[10]

Shakespeare's Sense of Fame as an Afterlife

The notion that one's posthumous reputation, informed by one's deeds and works accomplished while alive, constitutes an afterlife finds diverse expression in Shakespeare's work.

The Merchant of Venice, for example, invokes the idea that to affect the world during life is to enable an extension of life after death. During the trial scene, Antonio says to Bassanio:

> Commend me to your honourable wife.
> Tell her the process of Antonio's end.
> Say how I loved you. Speak me fair in death,
> And when the tale is told, bid her be judge

> Whether Bassanio had not once a love.
> Repent but you that you shall lose your friend,
> And he repents not that he pays your debt;
> For if the Jew do cut but deep enough,
> I'll pay it instantly, with all my heart. (4.1.270–8)

His speech brims with verbs in the imperative mood—"commend," "tell," "say," "speak," and "repent"—because he believes this to be his last opportunity to influence events in the world after he dies. Most of his injunctions involve demanding that he be kept alive in minds of others: spoken about in detail and spoken of positively. His reputation relies upon how other people will remember him in future discourse. In this play that constantly reminds us of the close connection between love and economics, we encounter a near-rhyme that links "debt" and "death." Antonio's loss of life will function as a final gift to his friend, who will "repent" his death by keeping him alive in the retelling of his sacrifice. The separation of these two friends should recall for us the separation of other characters—Caesar and Marc Antony, Suffolk, and York—where the loss of one represents a loss of an extension of the self, and where speaking about the lost friend, or pair of friends keeps them alive in the memory of others.

We encounter a case of reputation-as-afterlife with negative outcomes in *The Rape of Lucrece.* As he prepares to violate Lucrece, Tarquin relishes in the idea that her children's legitimacy will be in doubt after her rape. She, in turn, attempts to dissuade him by warning that his own reputation will live on as a testament to his crimes. When she says, "no outrageous thing / From vassal actors can be wiped away; / Then kings' misdeeds cannot be hid in clay," she reminds him that his actions will be set in stone within the larger cultural memory of him, even if he rises to become royalty (607–9). Although he will regret the crime, Tarquin does not desist in the face of this warning. Other Shakespearean villains share this trait of misjudging how their fame (as infamy) will be recorded. Cassius, for example, fantasizes that he and his fellow conspirators' acts will be performed on future stages such that "So often shall the knot of us be called / The men who gave their country liberty" (3.1.117–18). In the case of *Julius Caesar,* this knot of men has been recalled frequently in stagings of Shakespeare's play, but certainly not favorably.

In *Much Ado About Nothing,* Claudio delivers a speech that reads very much like an epitaph for his beloved Hero:

> Done to death by slanderous tongues
> Was Hero that here lies.
> Death in guerdon of her wrongs
> Gives her fame which never dies.
> So the life that died with shame
> Lives in death with glorious fame.
> *He hangs the epitaph on the tomb*
> Hang thou there upon the tomb,
> Praising her when I am dumb. (5.3.3–10)

We hear echoes here of ideas expressed in the commendatory poems to Shakespeare. The tomb should speak to the living and educate them, and this speech has the same function. Claudio desires for Hero's legacy to supersede the slander that he circulated just before she appeared to have died. While this may sound like a case of "too little, too late," it does serve two functions: to announce that she is destined for heaven given that she did not commit the sin of which she was accused, and to assuage Claudio's guilt as he now spreads word of Hero's virtue among the living. The scene of the repenting man who will encounter a seemingly resurrected lover presages the final moments of Shakespeare's later play *The Winter's Tale.* In Claudio's speech, he already wishes for Hero's extended life through "fame which never dies" in a gesture that foreshadows the revelation that she, like Hermione, will be given new life.

The Sonnets and the Promise of Immortality Through Friendship

Shakespeare's sonnets offer a particularly compelling case study for how writing was linked to immortality in the early modern period. In fact, we can locate within them a variety of formulations of an afterlife that might be realized through the acts of writing or reading the poems. On one level, several of the sonnets urge the addressee to have a child in order to "copy" himself and thus engender a form of extended life within his offspring. On another level, the sonnets themselves offer a form of immortality for the beloved to whom they are addressed because future generations will read about his beauty.

On yet another level, Shakespeare admits that these sonnets secure his own immortality as his writing will survive into the future.

The sonnets emphasize the aggressive passage of time in order to stress the need to think about what happens after death. Sonnet 19, for instance, counters "swift-footed time" with the notion that "My love shall in my verse ever live young" (19.6, 19.14). Sonnet 100 asks the muse to "Give my love fame faster than time wastes life; / So, thou prevene'st his scythe and crookèd knife" (100.13–4). This request articulates a calculus similar to that found within the commendatory poems quoted earlier. Reputation accrued while living can extend one's life beyond death. Yet the poem leaves it intriguingly ambiguous whether the "love" immortalized in verse will be the poet's emotion or the beloved toward whom that emotion is directed. In Sonnet 104, the speaker makes clear that it is his desire and his memory that fuel the beloved's immortality. The poem opens, "To me, fair friend, you never can be old; / For as you were when first your eye I eyed, / Such seems your beauty still" (104.1–3). The poem invests in mirroring, both in the sense that the eye reflects the beloved's beauty and in the sense that the poet can offer the best reflection of the speaker. Indeed, the poet himself is a reflection of the speaker as we see in the combination "eye I eyed." As Helen Vendler observes, "the acceleration in the pace of transience is enacted in the three transformations narrated" by the poem (winter shaking summer's pride, spring turned to autumn, and June burning April's perfumes).[11] Recall that transience was as the heart of Freud's formulation for mourning, as death reminds us about the fleeting qualities of the world. We might think of this sonnet as a scene of what scholars today term "anticipatory grief." The friend feels a sense of loss over what has not yet been lost to him. At the same time, the speaker does suggest that a fairer version of the addressee existed when he first spied him. Thus, the poem underscores the passing of time to make the friend feel a sense of urgency: he has already lost his best self who was in his prime. Across the sonnets, Shakespeare simultaneously articulates the problem of time's passing while he also suggests strategies to obviate that problem.

Several sonnets particularly foreground the notion that having a child offers a way to continue living. For example, Sonnet 3 warns its addressee, "Die single, and thine image dies with thee" (3.14). The use of "image" positions the child as a replica of the parent, and numerous puns on "die" throughout the sonnets suggest the child as cast from the original of the parent. Sonnet 7 puts in no uncertain terms the threat of time's passing and the need to recast oneself in a child: "So thou, thyself outgoing in thy noon, / Unlooked on diest unless thou get a son" (7.13–14). Sonnet 2 tempts the addressee with a sense of what it would be like to watch his child grow up: "This were to be new made when thou art old, / And see thy blood warm when thou feel'st it cold" (2.13–14). This reiterated message about the importance of having a child has led to the dubbing of the first seventeen sonnets as "the procreation sonnets." Paul Edmondson and Stanley Wells nicely describe the central concern as "re-creating the image of oneself in another living and autonomous being in order to combat the ravages of Time and so vicariously to achieve everlasting life."[12]

While these "procreation sonnets" urge the addressee to reproduce, this is not the only way in which he can live past his death. Shakespeare promises him immortality in the lines of the poems themselves. Sonnet 15, for example, declares that "for love of you, / [. . .] I engraft you new" (15.13–14). The lines conflate biological reproduction, where a small part of the parent plant can combine with another to form a new entity, with artistic production, where the poet reproduces his subject in verse. Desire for the beloved inspires Shakespeare both to imagine a child for the young man and to write about him. This interpretation relies on the double meaning of "engraft," which points both to the horticultural technique of grafting, and to writing as "graph," which derives from the ancient Greek term "*graphe*" meaning "to write." In the essay "Of Death," Francis Bacon writes that "Men fear death, as children fear to go in the dark; and as that natural fear in children is increased with tales, so is the other."[13] While his essay focuses primarily on the pains and discomforts that accompany death, it ends with a contemplation of how fame can help one live on. Indeed, death solves the problem of jealousy and allows others to engage in the praise necessary for continued life: "Death has this also; that it opens the gate to good fame, and extinguishes envy. *Extinctus amabitur idem* [The same man that was envied while he lived, shall be loved when he is gone]."[14] Shakespeare's sonnets offer to secure the enviable fame that Bacon's essay situates as a form of afterlife.

The notion that writing guarantees immortality appears across the sonnets in different ways. For example, Sonnet 18 promises eternal life for the addressee by comparing him to summer. Rather than evading winter by storing a bit of summer (as we see in Sonnet 4) or, by having a child, the addressee can move into a different temporal space entirely: eternity. The final four lines pointedly articulate this:

> Nor shall death brag thou wander'st in his shade
> When in eternal lines to time thou grow'st.
> So long as men can breathe or eyes can see,
> So long lives this, and this gives life to thee. (18.11–14)

The addressee will avoid the shadowy realm of death and also never become a "shade," using that term for ghost. While "eternal lines" might indicate genealogical lines, the "eternal lines" of the printed poem are what will keep him living. At the close of the poem, the alliteration ("lives," "life"; "this," thee"), rhyme ("lives," "gives"), and repetition ("this," this") emphasize the cyclical nature of time at the heart of eternity and also mirror the breathing of the living body. Whatever ambiguity might surround the phrase "eternal lines" in Sonnet 18, the closing line of Sonnet 19 makes things more explicit when it vows that "my love shall in my verse ever live young" (19.14). A reference to the "long-lived phoenix" in the poem underscores the poem as a meditation on resurrection (19.4).[15]

The multiple forms of doubling in the sonnets—where the child is a copy of the parent, and where the poem is a copy of its subject—come to the fore in the final couplet of Sonnet 17: "But were some child of yours alive that time, / You should live twice: in it, and in my rhyme" (17.13–14). In general, the last two lines of a sonnet gesture toward coupling in terms of the homophonic likeness between the end-words. Here, that rhyme suggests intimacy between the speaker and addressee. Jacques Derrida intriguingly suggests that the chime of rhyme has symbolic links to friendship, in part because it can be deployed to echo the ideals of likeness that undergird the bonds of amity. He posits that we can locate a "friendship of rhyme" within the literature of friendship, where instances of "alliance, harmony, assonance, chime" function as "traffic signals" for the presence of desire for connection between two people.[16] More than just vessels to extend the fame of the poet and his subject after their deaths, Shakespeare's poems emphasize that the memory of the friend will reside on the printed page and in the body of the friend who pens these sonnets. Sonnet 63 provides a useful flashpoint for the imbrication of friendship and immortality. Its final couplet connects the printed words of Shakespeare's poetry with the realization of eternal life:

> His beauty shall in these black lines be seen,
> And they shall live, and he in them still green. (63.13–14)

As Edmondson and Wells note, these lines instantiate the ways in which Shakespeare's poetic project is driven by "the will for immortality both of the verse and of the beloved."[17] Derrida, in his memorial essay for his friend and fellow philosopher Roland Barthes, suggests that the "best sign of fidelity" to the deceased friend is to "keep [the friend] alive, within oneself."[18] Thus, we can see the dual purpose of the sonnets. They keep the addressee alive in print while also emphasizing the speaker's love for him. Indeed, the two cannot easily be disaggregated. The writer must know the friend intimately to write about him. He must double him in print and be a double of him to write so compellingly about him.

Sonnet 29 and Sonnet 30 form a diptych that even more overtly positions friendship both as the inspiration for writing and as a means by which to achieve immortality. In Sonnet 29, the speaker begins "in disgrace" and "all alone" (29.1–2). The poet's state of misery at the start of the poem offers an instance of what Donne describes as "the manifold deaths of this *world*."[19] However, thoughts about the addressee allow the speaker to reach a state very much like heaven. He describes how "Haply I think on thee, and then my state, / Like to the lark at break of day arising / From sullen earth, sings hymns at heaven's gate" (29.10–12). This depiction of elevation leads Alan Bray to describe Sonnet 29 as "probably the most famous statement in all literature of that lifting of the spirit when the lover thinks of the beloved."[20] The "lifting of the spirit" here does not stem solely from solitary contemplation which improves the mood. The lover gains access to heavenly bliss only because the virtue of the friend takes him to new heights. The sonnet also links the melodies of poetry to the afterlife, especially as we recall that Orpheus was a figure linked to poetry in the early modern imagination and also linked to the ability to (almost) bring the dead back to life with the power of music. The way the speaker can ascend angel-like takes a religious formulation and puts it in service of secular forms of everlasting life. This returns us to a thread we have seen throughout this book where, as Eric S. Mallin puts it, "while the symbolic, thematic elements of Christianity certainly find their way into his work, Shakespeare activates these features in decidedly irreligious or ironic ways."[21] The angelic rise of the poet occurs while still living, as he writes about his beloved and appeals to join this friend's social circle.

Sonnet 30 also connects the lyricality of poetry to enhancing the spirit and even reviving deceased friends. The trope of resurrection as a source of joy recollects scenes we have seen in *Twelfth Night* and *The Winter's Tale,* while the earthly experience described in the sonnet recalls Schopenhauer's notion that reunion grants us a sense of what witnessing resurrection from the dead would actually feel like. The poem opens with the speaker grieving beloved friends whom he has lost. In his discussion of friendship, Derrida remarks that "*philia* begins with the possibility of survival. Surviving—that is the other name of a mourning whose possibility is never to be awaited."[22] That is, the desire for friendship is based partially in a desire that others will remember us, but these relationships run the risk of leaving us to lament missing friends. Here, the poet bemoans his separation from "precious friends hid in death's dateless night" (30.6).[23] Adam Phillips observes, "the world without the people who matter to us is not the same world, and so not the world at all."[24] This same estranging function of loss seems to motivate the poet to leave the present and escape into the realm of memory. Sonnet 30 opens with the famous lines, "When to the sessions of sweet silent thought / I summon up remembrance of things past" (30.2). The act of directing his gaze inward and backward can recall lost friends, and though he mourns them, the poet still brings them into the present. The final couplet ends the poem on an interestingly ambiguous note. It is not clear whether the new friend embodies the qualities of former friends, or if the old friends themselves have been replaced by the new one: "But if the while I think on thee, dear friend, / All losses are restored, and sorrows end" (30.13–14). As Helen Vendler notes, "no agency is ascribed to the young man" when "losses are restored and sorrows end."[25] Put another way, the speaker needs to think on his friend to feel complete, but he does not actually need this friend to be physically present.

By representing several, non-religious formulations of the afterlife, the sonnets ultimately rely on rendering the earthly future knowable. It is remarkable how little time is spent in the sonnets reiterating overtly Christian ideas and how much energy is invested in articulating strategies for outsmarting death. The consideration of the afterlife in the sonnets constitutes yet another example of how, as Eric S. Mallin puts it, "Shakespeare's beliefs, when they can be inferred, show a mind and a spirit uncontained by orthodoxy."[26] The poet reassures his beloved that he will mourn him and that his children will keep his memory alive after death. The poet, in turn, reassures himself that future readers will appreciate his writing about the beloved. Scheffler captures this dynamic nicely in his meditation on mortality when he frames our concerns about the afterlife as concern about how life will go on after us. For the dying or those contemplating death, "the world of the future becomes, as it were, more like a party one had to leave early and less like a gathering of strangers."[27] Yet the afterlife also draws meaning from the past. As Seana Valentine Shiffrin notes in a response to Scheffler, what makes the notion of a "rich collective afterlife" so compelling is that it "involves a continuation of the practices of valuing, if not the continuation of our actual values."[28] The larger enterprise of many of the sonnets relies upon the timelessness of the addressee's beauty, as well as the belief that the beauty of the lines written by the poet will be recognizable by generations of readers to come. Interestingly, we do not know today the identity of the person or persons to whom the sonnets might be addressed. We do, however, keep the poet alive in reverence of his art.

Endnotes

PREFACE

1. Billy Collins, "The Afterlife," *Poetry* (August 1990): 267–8, lines 4–5.
2. Collins, "The Afterlife," line 6.
3. My father's hospice care lasted for well over a year. As Karla Erickson notes in her study of contemporary experience of dying in the United States, it is not uncommon that families have long periods of time with the dying. "This kind of dying is protracted," she writes, "it is neither a time of dying nor a time of living as in other stages of life." In this peculiar middle-time, families and loved ones find themselves occupying a space very much "like standing on the threshold of a door frame between two rooms—one room is living without the spectre of dying, the other room is death itself." We will see that this threshold was certainly not unknown to early moderns. In fact, the theater brought audience members frequently into moments where individuals performed such waiting for death. Karla Erickson, *How We Die Now: Intimacy and the Work of Dying* (Philadelphia, PA: Temple University Press, 2013), 15.

INTRODUCTION

1. Alice Turner, *The History of Hell* (New York, NY: Harcourt Brace and Company, 1993), 162.
2. Counted using Open Source Shakespeare, https://www.opensourceshakespeare.org/concordance/.
3. In terms of Shakespeare, the nature of the afterlife is central to how we interpret some of the most famous elements of his work (e.g., the status of the ghosts, the repercussions for characters who commit suicide) and offers insights into religious debates of his time. It is worth noting that just as the supernatural can be found across works in the early modern period, figures and locations associated with the afterlife (e.g., ghosts, the undead, heaven, purgatory) are increasingly featured in television shows, film, and books that dominate our own popular culture.
4. David Scott Kastan, *A Will to Believe: Shakespeare and Religion* (New York, NY/Oxford: Oxford University Press, 2014), 15.

5. Schechner suggests that "social drama" (the ways in which actions in the social sphere draw upon elements of theatrical performance) is always in dialogue with "aesthetic drama" (the ways in which theater performance draws raw material from actions in the social sphere). He adopts the notion of "social drama" from Victor Turner and adds "aesthetic drama" as a component always in dialogue with the former. Both Schechner and Turner view the relationship between performance in the theater and performance in the social sphere as reciprocal, though Schechner interprets the two as being closer to equilibrium than does Turner. For the first formulation of this relationship as a diagram, see Richard Schechner, "Selective Inattention," in *Essays on Performance Theory 1970–1976* (New York, NY: Drama Books, 1977), 144. Steven Mullaney, *The Reformation of Emotions in the Age of Shakespeare* (Chicago, IL/London: University of Chicago Press, 2015), 7.
6. Mullaney, *Reformation of Emotions*, 7.
7. John Casey, *After Lives: A Guide to Heaven, Hell, & Purgatory* (Oxford/New York, NY: Oxford University Press, 2009), 20.
8. Sigmund Freud, "Mourning and Melancholy," *On Murder, Mourning, and Melancholy*, trans. Shaun Whiteside (New York, NY: Penguin, 2005), 214.
9. The authors take Freud's conception of melancholia as their point of departure, observing that "unlike mourning, in which the past is declared resolved, finished, and dead, in melancholia the past remains steadfastly alive in the present." David L. Eng and David Kazanjian, "Introduction: Mourning Remains," *Loss*, eds. David L. Eng and David Kazanjian (Berkeley, LA/London: University of California Press, 2003), 2 and 3–4.
10. Jacques Derrida, *Specters of Marx: The State of Debt, The Work of Mourning, and the New International*, trans. Peggy Kamuf (New York, NY/London: Routledge, 1994), 113.
11. Mullaney, *Reformation of Emotions*, 10.
12. Indeed, we might ask why a father has stronger influence from the afterlife than a living father with the same desires in *A Midsummer Night's Dream*.
13. In one of many cases where psychoanalysts have turned to Shakespeare to explain their theories, Freud uses Prince Hamlet as an example in this same essay. Freud, "Mourning and Melancholy," 204.
14. Freud, "Mourning and Melancholy," 204.
15. Freud, "Transience," *On Murder, Mourning, and Melancholy*, 200.
16. Judith Butler, *Undoing Gender* (New York, NY/London: Routledge, 2004), 20–1.
17. Jacques Derrida, *Specters of Marx*, trans. Peggy Kamuf (Abingdon/New York, NY, 1994), 121.

CHAPTER 1

1. Francis Bacon, "Of Atheism," *Francis Bacon: The Major Works*, ed. Brian Vickers (Oxford: Oxford University Press, 2008), 372.
2. Donne, "Death's Duel. Preached before Charles I (February 25, 1631)," *The Major Works: Including Songs and Sonnets and Sermons* (Oxford: Oxford University Press, 2009), 410.
3. Donne, "Death's Duel. Preached before Charles I (February 25, 1631)," *Major Works*, 410.
4. *Martin Luther, Martin Luther's Table Talk: Abridged from Luther's Works, Volume 54,* ed. Henry F. French (Minneapolis, MN:Fortress Press, 2017), 54, 297.
5. The title of More's volume refers to death, judgment, heaven, and hell, which comprise the objects of study of *eschatology*. Thomas More, *The Four Last Things*, ed. D. O'Connor (London/Leamington: Art and Book Company, 1903), 93.
6. Laurie E. Maguire and Emma Smith, *30 Great Myths About Shakespeare* (Malden/Oxford: Wiley-Blackwell, 2013), 48.
7. B. J. Sokol, *Shakespeare and Tolerance* (Cambridge: Cambridge University Press, 2009), 59.
8. George Santayana, *Interpretations of Poetry and Religion* (New York, NY: C. Scribner's Sons, 1900), 152.
9. Santayana, *Interpretations of Poetry and Religion*, 152.
10. Cynthia Marshall, *Last Things and Last Plays: Shakespearean Eschatology* (Carbondale, IL: Southern Illinois University Press, 1991), 5–6.
11. Eric S. Mallin, *Godless Shakespeare* (London/New York, NY: Continuum, 2007), 1.
12. The phrase "what dreams may come" is repurposed as the title of one of the better-known films about the afterlife. The 1998 *What Dreams May Come* (dir. Vincent Ward), based on a 1978 novel of the same name by Richard Matheson, stars Robin Williams as a pediatrician who traverses heaven and hell in search of his wife who has committed suicide.
13. Donne, *Major Works*, 13.
14. Sasha Handley, *Sleep in Early Modern England* (New Haven, CT: Yale University Press 2016), 82.
15. Martin Luther, *Table Talk* 180.
16. Donne, *Major Works*, 176.
17. Thomas More, *The Four Last Things*, 36.
18. Ludwig Lavater, *Of Ghosts and Spirits Walking by Night and of Strange Noises, Cracks, and Sundry Forewarnings*, trans. R. H. (London: Henry Benneyman, 1572), 117.

19. Casey, *After Lives*, 13.
20. Lynn Enterline, *Shakespeare's Schoolroom: Rhetoric, Discipline, Emotion* (Philadelphia, PA: University of Pennsylvania Press, 2012), 9.
21. Frances Yates, *Giordano Bruno and the Hermetic Tradition* (Chicago, IL: University of Chicago Press, 1964), vi.
22. Luther, *Table Talk*, 180.
23. In fact, the space of forgetting may have sounded much like a place of bliss. In the *Phaedo*, Plato posits that a soul can "make its way to the invisible, which is like itself, the divine and immortal and wise, and arriving there it can be happy, having rid itself of confusion, ignorance, fear, violent desires, and the other human ills." Plato, *Complete Works*, eds. John M. Cooper and D. S. Hutchinson (Indianapolis, IN/Cambridge: Hackett Publishing Company, 1997), 71.
24. Glenn Wickham, "Hell-Castle and its Doorway," *Shakespeare Survey* 19 (1966): 73.
25. Aristotle, *Poetics*, trans. Gerald Else (Ann Arbor, MI: University of Michigan Press, 1967), 38, sec. 531a.
26. Blair Hoxby, *What Was Tragedy?: Theory and the Early Modern Canon* (Oxford: Oxford University Press, 2015), 8.
27. Jonathan Gil Harris traces other resonances of the Gunpowder Plot—ranging from the witches' "fair" and "foul" echoing a sermon by Lancelot Andrewes about the Plot, to the smoke of hell echoing King James' speech about the traitors being condemned to smoke and fiery afterlives—to find that "even though the plot is never alluded to directly, then, its presence is everywhere in the play." Jonathan Gil Harris, *Untimely Matter in the Age of Shakespeare* (Philadelphia, PA: University of Pennsylvania Press, 2011), 126. See also Rebecca Lemon, "Scaffolds of Treason in *Macbeth*," *Theatre Journal* 54.1 (2002): 25–43.
28. Nick Moschovakis, "Introduction: Dualistic *Macbeth*? Problematic *Macbeth*?," *Macbeth: New Critical Essays*, ed. Nick Moschovakis (London/New York, NY: Routledge, 2008), 6.
29. *The Oxford Companion to Shakespeare*, eds. Michael Dobson and Stanley Wells (Oxford: Oxford University Press, 2001), 359.
30. Ewan Fernie, *The Demonic: Literature and Experience* (London: Routledge, 2012), 51.
31. Erickson, *How We Die Now*, 177.
32. Special thanks to Jan Frans van Dijkheizen for pointing me towards this excerpt. Folger MS V.a.248.
33. Carol Zaleski, *Otherworld Journeys: Accounts of Near-Death Experience in Medieval and Modern Times* (New York, NY: Oxford University Press, 1987), 48.

34. Donne, "Death's Duel. Preached before Charles I (February 25, 1631)," *Major Works*, 410.
35. Kristen Poole, *Supernatural Environments in Shakespeare's England: Spaces of Demonism, Divinity, and Drama* (Cambridge: Cambridge University Press, 2011), 64.
36. Poole, *Supernatural Environments*, 84.
37. Ramie Targoff, *Posthumous Love: Eros and the Afterlife in Renaissance England* (Chicago, IL: University of Chicago Press, 2014), 107.
38. As she and her women decide to pursue suicide, Cleopatra asks, "is it sin / To rush into the secret house of death / Ere death come to us?" (4.16.83–5). The lines echo those claims by Claudio and Hamlet that the afterlife is unknowable. The use of the term "house" parallels King Hamlet's exclamation that "I am forbid / To tell the secrets of my prison-house" (1.5.14). The use of "house" uses earthly terms to describe the unearthly. A passage in 2 Corinthians 5:1 reads "For we know that if our earthly dwelling, a tent, should be destroyed, we have a building from God, a dwelling not made with hands, eternal in heaven." Here, too, we can only understand the "life to come" in terms of the life currently lived.
39. Michael MacDonald and Terence R. Murphy, *Sleepless Souls: Suicide in Early Modern England* (Oxford: Oxford University Press, 2002), 6.
40. MacDonald and Murphy, *Sleepless Souls*, 5.
41. MacDonald and Murphy, *Sleepless Souls*, 94.
42. R. A. Houston, *Punishing the Dead?: Suicide, Lordship, and Community in Britain, 1500–1830* (Oxford: Oxford University Press, 2011), 190–1.
43. Cited in Paul S. Seaver, "Suicide and the Vicar General in London: A Mystery Solved?," in *From Sin to Insanity: Suicide in Early Modern Europe*, ed. Jeffrey R. Watt (Ithaca, NY: Cornell University Press, 2004), 27.
44. Paul Seaver's study on the subject notes, a jury "could obviate the sanctions imposed on homicides, including suicides," and between 1610 and 1641, the diocese of London granted thirty-one licenses that allowed Christian burials for those who committed suicide. Seaver, 26.
45. John Donne, *Biathanatos* (London, 1647).
46. Ramie Targoff, *John Donne: Body and Soul* (Chicago, IL: University of Chicago Press, 2008), 151.
47. Mullaney, *Reformation of Emotions*, 167.
48. Michael Neill, *Issues of Death: Mortality and Identity in English Renaissance Tragedy* (Oxford: Oxford University Press, 1997), 71.
49. Hans Holbein's illustrated "Dance of Death Alphabet" (1524), which features 24 letters as historiated initials, embeds death itself directly into language. Each letter shows death attempting to seize an individual. We

might read this as language's attempt to ward off death or as death's power to overwhelm language.

50. Daniel Pickering Walter, *The Decline of Hell: Seventeenth-Century Discussions of Eternal Torment* (Chicago, IL: University of Chicago Press, 1964).
51. Peter Marshall, "'The map of God's word': Geographies of the Afterlife in Tudor and Early Stuart England," *The Place of the Dead: Death and Remembrance in Late Medieval and Early Modern Europe*, eds. Bruce Gordon and Peter Marshall (Cambridge/New York, NY: Cambridge University Press, 2000), 110–11.
52. Targoff, *Posthumous Love*, 4.
53. Paul Morrison, "*Measure for Measure:* Same-Saint Desire," in *Shakesqueer: A Queer Companion to the Complete Works of William Shakespeare*, ed. Madhavi Menon (Durham/London: Duke University Press, 2011), 210.
54. Michel de Montaigne, *The Complete Essays*, trans. M. A. Screech (New York, NY: Penguin, 1993), 103.
55. Montaigne, *Complete Essays*, 96.
56. Sarah Beckwith, *Shakespeare and the Grammar of Forgiveness* (Ithaca, NY: Cornell University Press, 2002), 59.
57. Isabella's use of "perpetual durance" echoes the notion in *Richard III* that death propels an individual into a "kingdom of perpetual night" (1.4.48). Imprisonment may also share with death what Donne describes as "dissolution and dispersion" and "peremptory nullification" of the self after death. John Donne, "Death's Duel," in *Devotions Upon Emergent Occasions Together with Death's Duel* (Ann Arbor, MI: University of Michigan Press, 1959), 176–7.
58. Karmen MacKendrick, *Counterpleasures* (Albany, NY: State University of New York Press, 1999), 158.
59. Her claim builds on the work of Bataille, who asserts that "If you die, it is not my death. You and I are *discontinuous* beings." MacKendrick helps us see how death, while ultimately the force that can separate individuals and that stresses their state as "discontinuous" with each other, also functions to bind individuals through the shared expectation of one's death. Georges Bataille, *Erotism: Death and Sensuality*, trans. Mary Dalwood (San Francisco, CA: City Lights Books, 1957), 12, and MacKendrick, *Counterpleasures*, 159.
60. Bataille, *Erotism: Death and Sensuality*, 11.
61. We see this sentiment also in *Cymbeline*, where a song tells us, "Golden lads and girls all must, / As chimney-sweepers, come to dust" (4.2.263–4). It would seem to be our destiny but also our assigned work to be born, to live, to die, and to dissipate.

62. John Donne counterposes the immortality of the soul to the transience of the body in the same terms. He describes the state of bodily decay as one "where the worms that we breed are our betters, because they have a life, where the dust of dead kings is blown into the street, and the dust of the street blown into the river, and the muddy river tumbled into the sea, and the sea remanded into all the veins and channels of the earth." John Donne, *John Donne: Selections from Divine Poems, Sermons, Devotions, and Prayers*, ed. John Booty (Mahwah, NJ: Paulist Press, 1990), 162.
63. Ernest Hemingway, *A Farewell to Arms* (New York, NY: Scribner, 2014), 122.
64. Mallin, *Godless Shakespeare*, 8.
65. Jonathan Dollimore, *Death, Desire, and Loss in Western Culture* (New York, NY: Routledge, 1998), 115. In miniature, we can see the relationship between life and death (one as the absence of the other) in our unfulfilled goals and unattained riches.
66. Victoria Bladen and Marcus Harmes, "Introduction: The intersections of Supernatural and Secular Power," in *Supernatural and Secular Power in Early Modern England*, eds. Marcus Harmes and Victoria Bladen (Farnham/Burlington, VT: Ashgate Publishing, 2015), 3.
67. Dollimore, *Death, Desire, and Loss*, 114.
68. Julia Reinhard Lupton, *Citizen-Saints: Shakespeare and Political Theology* (Chicago, IL: University of Chicago Press, 2005), 145.
69. Leo Bersani, "The Power of Evil and the Power of Love," in Leo Bersani and Adam Phillips, *Intimacies* (Chicago, IL: University of Chicago Press, 2010), 67.
70. Robert N. *The Rest is Silence: Death as Annihilation in the English Renaissance* (Berkeley, CA/London: University of California Press, 1994), 121.

CHAPTER 2

1. Martin Luther, "Whether One May Flee from a Deadly Plague," in *Luther's Works*, ed. and trans. Theodore G. Tappert (Philadelphia, PA: Fortress Press, 1967), section 42.137.
2. Elizabeth I's 1560 proclamation extending this statute is reproduced by the antiquary John Weever in his *Ancient Funeral Monuments* (London: Thomas Harper, 1631), 52–4.
3. I thank Dustin Dixon for helping me think through the ancient Greek etymologies here. The term "*soma*" replaces "*sema*" in ancient texts by Strabo and the Pseudo Callisthenes. For a discussion of the interchangeability of the terms, see the editor's commentary in Strabo, *The Geography of Strabo*, Vol. 8,

ed. Horace Leonard Jones (Cambridge/London: Harvard University Press, 1932), 37n48.

4. Scott Newstok, *Quoting Death in Early Modern England: The Poetics of Epitaphs Beyond the Tomb* (New York, NY/London: Palgrave Macmillan, 2009), 17.
5. Keith Thomas, *The Ends of Life: Roads to Fulfilment in Early Modern England* (Oxford/New York, NY: Oxford University Press, 2009), 249–50.
6. Peter Shylock's *Monuments and Memory in Early Modern England* (Farnham/ Burlington, VT: Ashgate Publishing, 2008) offers an excellent overview of the topic. Also see Scott Newstok, *Quoting Death in Early Modern England: The Poetics of Epitaphs Beyond the Tomb* (New York, NY: Palgrave Macmillan, 2009), and Joshua Scodel's *The English Poetic Epitaph: Commemoration and Conflict from Jonson to Wordsworth* (Ithaca, NY: Cornell University Press, 1991), which both focus on literary representations of epitaphs. These two books offer insightful interpretations of epitaphs included in poetry by canonical authors such as Shakespeare, Milton, and others who use the epitaph form as a way to express lament in their printed works.
7. George Herbert, *The Complete English Poems*, ed. John Tobin (New York, NY: Penguin, 1991), 58–9.
8. Nigel Llewellyn, *Funeral Monuments in Post-Reformation England* (Cambridge/New York, NY: Cambridge University Press, 2009), 8.
9. Vanessa Harding, *The Dead and the Living in Paris and London, 1500–1670* (Cambridge: Cambridge University Press, 2002), 83.
10. Joseph Roach, *Cities of the Dead: Circum-Atlantic Performance* (New York, NY: Columbia University Press, 1996), 48. See also 47–55.
11. Mario Erasmo, *Death: Antiquity and its Legacy* (Oxford/New York, NY: Oxford University Press, 2012), 108.
12. Poussin's 1627 version of the painting shows a different tomb but with the same inscription.
13. Armando Petrucci, *Writing the Dead: Death and Writing Strategies in the Western Tradition*, trans. Michael Sullivan (Stanford, CA: Stanford University Press, 1998), 96.
14. Newstok, *Quoting Death*, 21.
15. All references to biblical passages in this volume refer to the 1599 Geneva Bible.
16. Susan Zimmerman, *The Early Modern Corpse and Shakespeare's Theatre* (Edinburgh: Edinburgh University Press, 2005), 1–2.
17. Matthew 8:11 and Luke 13:28 suggest that one unites with biblical worthies in heaven. So, perhaps Arthur represents a divine worthy figure for Falstaff.
18. Philippe Ariès, *The Hour of Our Death: The Classic History of Western Attitudes Toward Death over the Last One Thousand Years* (New York, NY: Vintage Books, 1982), 603.

19. Ramie Targoff opens her volume *Posthumous Love: Eros and the Afterlife* with a description of a spousal tomb in Rome which depicts a married couple reunited in heaven. Similarly, the discovery of numerous tombs in Cambridge that depict same-sex friends joined in the afterlife ignites Alan Bray's wonderful study *The Friend.* Alan Bray, *The Friend* (Chicago, IL: University of Chicago Press, 2003), 1–5.
20. John Dunton, *Essay Proving We Shall Know Our Friends in Heaven* (London: E. Whitlock, 1698), 4 (A2v).
21. See John Garrison, "Shakespeare and Friendship: An Intersection of Interest." *Literature Compass* 9.5 (May 2012): 371–9.
22. For details on the partnership between and deaths of Neville and Clanvowe, see Bray, *The Friend*, 32–41.
23. *The Westminster Chronicle* is believed to have been co-authored by two monks, though one seems to have taken over as the sole author at the end of 1383. See *The Westminster Chronicle: 1381–994*, edited and translated by L. C. Hector and Barbara F. Harvey (Oxford: Clarendon Press, 1982), xiii–xiv and 480–1.
24. David L. Eng and David Kazanjian, "Introduction: Mourning Remains," in *Loss: The Politics of Mourning*, eds. David L. Eng and David Kazanjian (Berkeley, CA/London: University of California Press, 2003), 2.
25. See Alastair Fowler, *Time's Purpled Masquers: Stars and the Afterlife in Renaissance English Literature* (Oxford: Clarendon Press, 1996).
26. Julia Kristeva, *Tales of Love*, trans. Leon S. Roudiez (New York, NY: Columbia University Press, 1987), 210.
27. Denis De Rougemont, *Love in the Western World*, trans. Montgomery Belgion (Princeton, NJ: Princeton University Press, 1983), 46.
28. 1548. qtd in Hoxby, *Tragedy*, p. 103.
29. Samuel Pepys, *The Diary of Samuel Pepys*, ed. Richard Le Galienne (New York, NY: The Modern Library, 2003), 299 (entry for February 23, 1669).
30. Dollimore, *Death, Desire, and Loss*, 109.
31. Kristeva, *Tales of Love*, 215.
32. Targoff, *Posthumous Love*, 127.
33. Mario Erasmo, *Death: Antiquity and Its Legacy* (I.B. Tauris & Co. Ltd, 2012, 74–84.
34. John Webster, *The Duchess of Malfi*, ed. Brian Gibbons (London/New York, NY: Bloomsbury Methuen Drama, 2014), 5.3.38–40.
35. John Ford, *Love's Sacrifice*, ed. A. T. Moore (Manchester: Manchester University Press, 2002), 56.55–6.
36. Andrew Stark, *The Consolations of Morality: Making Sense of Death* (New Haven, CT: Yale University Press, 2016), 34.

37. Colin Burrow, *Shakespeare and Classical Antiquity* (Oxford: Oxford University Press), 117.
38. Roland Barthes, *A Lover's Discourse: Fragments*, trans. Richard Howard (New York, NY: Hill and Wang, 1978), 74.
39. Jan Frans van Dijkhuizen, "Partakers of Pain: Religious Meanings of Pain in Early Modern England," in *The Sense of Suffering: Constructions of Physical Pain in Early Modern Culture*, eds. Jan Frans van Dijkhuizen and Karl A. E. Enenkel (Leiden: Brill, 2009), 203.
40. Stanley Wells, *Shakespeare, Sex, and Love* (Oxford: Oxford University Press, 2010), 216.
41. Arthur Schopenhauer, *Studies in Pessimism* (Whitefish, MT: Kessinger Publishing, 2010), 65.
42. John Woolton, *A New Anatomy of Whole Man, as well of his Body, of his Soule* (London: 1576), 42v.
43. *The Book of Common Prayer: The Texts of 1549, 1559, and 1662*, ed. Brian Cummings (Oxford: Oxford University Press, 2011), 66.
44. Targoff, *Posthumous Love*, 30.
45. All quotations from *Aeneid* are drawn from Virgil, *Aeneid*, trans. Elaine Fatham (Oxford: Oxford University Press, 2008).
46. Lauren Berlant, *Cruel Optimism* (Durham, NC: Duke University Press, 2011), 20.
47. David Scott Kastan, *A Will to Believe: Shakespeare and Religion* (New York, NY/Oxford: Oxford University Press, 2014), 15.
48. Peter Marshall, "'The map of God's word': Geographies of the Afterlife in Tudor and Early Stuart England," in *The Place of the Dead: Death and Remembrance in Late Medieval and Early Modern Europe*, eds. Bruce Gordon and Peter Marshall (Cambridge/New York, NY: Cambridge University Press, 2000), 110–11.
49. Adam Phillips, *Unforbidden Pleasures: Rethinking Authority, Power, and Authority* (New York, NY: Farrar, Straus, and Giroux, 2016), 61.
50. Targoff, *Posthumous Love*, 132.
51. Phillips, *Unforbidden Pleasures*, 105.
52. Wells, *Shakespeare, Sex, and Love*, 216.

CHAPTER 3

1. *Hamlet*, dir. Gregory Doran, filmed adaptation of a Royal Shakespeare Company production (BBC Wales, Illuminations, NHK Enterprises, Royal Shakespeare Company, and WNET, 2009).
2. To answer "yes" to this question might also be to affirm Freud's notion (discussed in the Introduction) that mourning is at heart a process of readying oneself for a replacement object of desire.

3. *Hamlet*, dir. Michael Almereyda (Double A Films, 2000).
4. Christopher Marlowe, *Doctor Faustus, A-Text, Doctor Faustus and Other Plays*, eds. David Bevington and Eric Rasmussen (Oxford: Oxford University Press, 1998), 1.3.77.
5. Ariès, *The Hour of Our Death*, x.
6. Frances E. Dolan, "Hermione's Ghost: Catholicism, the Feminine, and the Undead," *The Impact of Feminism in English Renaissance Studies*, ed. Dympna Callaghan (London/New York, NY: Palgrave, 2007), 222.
7. Dolan notes their argument on pages 223–4 of her discussion. Ann Jones and Peter Stallybrass, *Renaissance Clothing and the Materials of Memory* (Cambridge: Cambridge University Press, 2000), 245–68.
8. Dolan, "Hermione's Ghost," 224.
9. See Douglas Iain Clark, "The Will and Testamentary Eroticism in Shakespearean Drama," *Sexuality and Memory in Early Modern England: Literature and the Erotics of Recollection*, eds. John S. Garrison and Kyle Pivetti (London/New York, NY: Routledge, 2015), 30–42, esp. 33–5.
10. Jacques Derrida, *Spectres of Marx* (Routledge, 1994), 25.
11. Stanley Wells, "Staging Shakespeare's Ghosts," in Stanley Wells, *Shakespeare on Page and Stage: Selected Essays*, ed. Paul Edmondson (Oxford: Oxford University Press, 2016), 262.
12. Cicero, *Laelius, On Friendship (Laelius de Amicitia) & The Dream of Scipio*, trans. J. G. F. Powell (Warminster: Aris and Phillips Ltd., 1990), sec. 1.25.
13. Cicero, *Laelius, On Friendship*, sec. 21.
14. Bacon, *The Major Works*, 395.
15. "Ghost" continues to function as a generalized sign of disturbance. As the play rushes towards it conclusion, Cassius announces that "Our army lies ready to give ghost," implying not only how war is always haunted by death but also how the army renders the individual anonymous in a larger group as a single "ghost" accounts for the deaths of many.
16. The "future history" play, Mike Bartlett's *King Charles III* (2014), is set in the near-future when the current Prince Charles becomes king of England. It is written largely in the iambic pentameter of an early modern play, and true to the genre, it features a ghost. Princess Diana appears as a phantom who haunts the royal palace.
17. Hester Lees-Jeffries, *Shakespeare and Memory* (Oxford: Oxford University Press, 2013), 81.
18. Peter Buse and Andrew Stott, "Introduction: A Future for Haunting," *Ghosts: Deconstruction, Psychoanalysis, History*, eds. Peter Buse and Andrew Stott (Houndsmills: Macmillan, 1999), 10.
19. Carlos Eire, *A Very Brief History of Eternity* (Princeton, NJ: Princeton University Press, 2010), 25.

20. Eire, *Brief History of Eternity*, 25.
21. Michel Foucault, "Of Other Spaces," trans. Jay Miskowiec, *Diacritics* 16 (Spring 1986): 25.
22. Foucault, "Of Other Spaces," 25.
23. Roger Lockhurst, "'Something Tremendous, Something Elemental': On the Ghostly Origins of Psychoanalysis," *Ghosts: Deconstruction, Psychoanalysis, History*, 62.
24. Martin Luther, "On the Misuse of the Mass," *Luther's Works*, eds. Jaroslav Pelikan *et al.* (Philadelphia, PA: Muhlenberg Press, 1955–1986), Vol. 36, 91.
25. Arthur F. Kinney, *Shakespeare's Webs: Networks of Meaning in Renaissance Drama* (London/New York, NY: Routledge, 2004), 50.
26. Jacques Le Goff, *The Birth of Purgatory*, trans. Arthur Goldhammer (Chicago, IL: University of Chicago Press, 1986), 36.
27. Mullaney, *Reformation of Emotions*, 10.
28. Stephen Greenblatt, *Hamlet in Purgatory* (Princeton, NJ: Princeton University Press, 2001), 256.
29. Eire, *Brief History of Eternity*, 110–11.
30. Disney's 1994 animated adaptation of *Hamlet, The Lion King* (dir. Roger Allers and Rob Mikoff) stresses this likeness when the young prince (Simba) stares at his own reflection in the water before it becomes the face of his father (Mufasa) just before the encounter with the ghost that will urge him to "remember who you are." The idea that the child should replicate the father is one we see across Shakespeare's work, including the use of the word "copy" in the *Sonnets* and "a form in wax" in *A Midsummer Night's Dream* to refer to children.
31. Richard Kearney, "Spectres of *Hamlet*," *Spiritual Shakespeares*, ed. Ewan Fernie (Abingdon/New York, NY: Routledge, 2005), 184.
32. Hester Lees-Jeffries, *Shakespeare and Memory* (Oxford University Press, 2013), 104.
33. Roland Barthes, *Mourning Diary*, trans. Richard Howard (New York, NY: Hill and Wang, 2010), 179.
34. Dolan, "Hermione's Ghost," 214.
35. Greenblatt, *Hamlet in Purgatory*, 249.
36. Bert O. States, *Hamlet and the Concept of Character* (Baltimore, MD: Johns Hopkins University Press, 1992), 7.
37. Michelle O'Callaghan, "Dreaming the Dead: Ghosts and History in the Early Seventeenth Century," *Reading the Early Modern Dream: The Terrors of the Night*, eds. Katharine Hodgkin, Michelle O'Callaghan, and S. J. Wiseman (London: Routledge, 2008), 81.
38. O'Callaghan, "Dreaming the Dead," 82.
39. Adam Phillips, *Side Effects* (London/New York, NY: Penguin, 2006), 104.

40. Carolyn Dinshaw, *How Soon is Now? Medieval Texts, Amateur Readers, and the Queerness of Time* (Durham: Duke University Press, 2012), 4.
41. Phillips, *Side Effects*, 104.
42. Christine Varnado, "Queer Nature, or the Weather in *Macbeth*," *Queer Shakespeare: Desire and Sexuality*, ed. Goran Stanivukovic (London/New York, NY: Bloomsbury Arden Shakespeare, 2017), 183.
43. Varnado, "Queer Nature," 183.
44. Fernie, *The Demonic: Literature and Experience*, 52.
45. Francis Beaumont, *The Knight of the Burning Pestle*, ed. Michael Hattaway (London/New York, NY: Bloomsbury Methuen Drama, 2002).
46. Raphael Lyne, *Shakespeare's Late Work* (Oxford: Oxford University Press, 2007), 123.
47. Simon Palfrey, "Macbeth and Kierkegaard," *Shakespeare Survey* 57, *Macbeth and Its Afterlife: An Annual Survey*, ed. Peter Holland (Cambridge: Cambridge University Press, 2008), 108.
48. Heather Love, "Milk," *Shakesqueer: A Queer Companion to the Complete Works of William Shakespeare*, ed. Madhavi Menon (Durham: Duke University Press, 2011), 201.
49. O'Callaghan, "Dreaming the Dead," 49.
50. Because the figures who accompany Banquo will be dead by the time Shakespeare composes this play, they constitute the promise of future ghosts and of the long cycle of death that Richard II and Timon see in the dynamics of war and kingship. Such a cycle of haunting and revenge finds expression when Macduff exclaims that if Macbeth is "slain and with no stroke of mine, / My wife and children's ghosts will haunt me still" (5.8.2–3).
51. Catherine Stevens, "You shal reade mavellous straunge things": Ludwig Lavater and The Hauntings of the Reformation, in *Supernatural and Secular Power*, eds. Marcus Harmes and Victoria Bladen (Farnham/Burlington, VT: Ashgate Publishing, 2015), 143.
52. Stephen Greenblatt, *Shakespearean Negotiations: The Circulation of Social Energy in Renaissance England* (Berkeley, CA: University of California Press, 1989), 1.
53. Greenblatt, *Hamlet in Purgatory*, 108.
54. Russ McDonald, *Shakespeare and the Arts of Language* (Oxford: Oxford University Press, 2001), 160.
55. McDonald, *Shakespeare and the Arts of Language*, 160.
56. They serve a function here like the perspective of the aged John of Gaunt, who in his famous speech about England as a "sceptered isle" laments what the country has become.
57. Watson, *Death as Annihilation*, 142.
58. Eire, *A Very Brief History of Eternity*, 14.

CHAPTER 4

1. William N. West, "Replaying Early Modern Performances," *New Directions in Renaissance Drama and Performance Studies*, ed. Sarah Werner (Houndmills/New York, NY: Palgrave Macmillan, 2010), 35.
2. Qtd. in Marisa R. Cull, *Shakespeare's Princes of Wales: English Identity and the Welsh Connection* (Oxford: Oxford University Press, 2014), 67. The passage appears in Raphael Holinshed, *The Third Volume of the Chronicles* (London: 1586), 528.
3. Joseph Roach, "History, Memory, Necrophilia," *The Ends of Performance*, eds. Peggy Phelan and Jill Lane (New York, NY: New York University Press, 1998), 29.
4. W. Vaughan, *The Golden-Grove Moralized in Three Books* (London: Simon Stafford, 1600), Y8v.
5. Vaughn, *Golden-Grove*, Y8v.
6. Christopher Highley, "Wales, Ireland, and *1 Henry IV*," in *Renaissance Drama 21: Disorder and the Drama*, ed. Mary Beth Rose (Evanston, IL: Northwestern University Press, 1991), 99.
7. Arthur Schopenhauer, *Studies in Pessimism* (Whitefish, MT: Kessinger Publishing, 2010), 65.
8. Viola later explains that "Sebastian was my father. / Such a Sebastian was my brother, too" (5.1.230–1). The statement nods to how the child can be an afterlife for the parent, as particularly emphasized in the Sonnets explored further in the next chapter.
9. Dollimore, *Death, Desire, and Loss*, 68.
10. Mallin, *Godless Shakespeare*, 110.
11. Dolan, "Hermione's Ghost," 224.
12. Beckwith, *Shakespeare and the Grammar of Forgiveness*, 142.
13. Colin Burrow, *Shakespeare and Classical Antiquity* (Oxford: Oxford University Press, 2013), 127.
14. Marjorie B. Garber, *Shakespeare After All* (New York, NY: Pantheon Books, 2004), 847.
15. Earlier in the play, Antigonus meets Hermione's ghost in a dream, "gasping to begin some speech" as she reveals Perdita's name to him (3.3.24). This provides another instance of a desire to hear the dead speak. As in *Hamlet* and elsewhere, this ghost will not speak of the afterlife but rather has come to share revelations about the living world.
16. Meres, *Palladis Tamia* (1598), qtd in *The Bedford Companion to Shakespeare: An Introduction with Documents*, ed. Russ McDonald (London/New York, NY: Palgrave, 2001), 32.

17. Sean Benson, *Shakespearean Resurrection: The Art of Almost Raising the Dead* (Pittsburgh, PA: Duquesne University Press, 2009), 182.
18. All references to Golding's translation draw from the Perseus Digital Library. Arthur Golding (1567), *Ovid. Metamorphoses*, London: W. Seres, in the *Perseus Digital Library*, ed. Gregory R. Crane. Tufts University, http://www.perseus.tufts.edu/hopper/ (last accessed December 10, 2016).
19. Melissa E. Sanchez, "Seduction and Service in *The Tempest*," *Studies in Philology* 105 (2008): 52.
20. Margreta de Grazia observes that Prospero's magic is "hardly distinguishable from that of Caliban's mother Sycorax," thus further encouraging us to collapse absent women into his actions and his rhetoric. Margreta de Grazia, "*The Tempest*: Gratuitous Movement or Action without Kibes and Pinches," *Shakespeare Studies* 14 (1981): 55.
21. For a discussion of how Portia's character parallels Medea and even echoes some of her lines from Ovid, see Michael Zuckert, "The New Medea: On Portia's Comic Triumph in *The Merchant of Venice*," in *Shakespeare's Political Pageant: Essays in Literature and Politics*, eds. Joseph Alulis and Dennis Bathory (New York, NY: Rowman and Littlefield, 1996), 3–36.
22. Philip Sidney, "Sonnet 1," in *The Norton Anthology of English Literature 9th Edition, Volume B: The Sixteenth Century and the Early Seventeenth Century*, eds. Stephen Greenblatt, Katharine Eisaman Maus, George Logan, and Barbara K. Lewalski (New York, NY/London: W.W. Norton and Company, 2012), 1084.
23. Barbara A. Mowat, "Prospero's Book," *Shakespeare Quarterly* 52.1 (Spring 2001): 29.
24. Beckwith, *Grammar of Forgiveness*, 160.
25. Stephen Orgel, "Prospero's Wife," *Representations* 8 (Autumn 1984): 11.
26. All references to Ovid's Latin draw from the Loeb edition. Shakespeare draws upon both Golding's English version and Ovid's Latin. For a discussion of prior scholarly work on this, see Gordon Braden, "Ovid's Witchcraft," *Reception and the Classics: An Interdisciplinary Approach to the Classical Tradition*, eds. William Brockliss, Pramit Chaudhuri, Ayelet Haimson Lushkov, and Katherine Wasdin (Cambridge/New York, NY: Cambridge University Press, 2012), 128. Ovid, *Metamorphoses: Books I–VIII*, trans. Frank Justus Miller and G. P. Goold (Cambridge/London: Harvard University Press, 1977).
27. Roland Barthes, *Writing Degree Zero*, trans. Annette Lavers and Colin Smith (New York, NY: Hill and Wang, 1977), 9.

28. Barthes, *Writing Degree Zero*, 10.
29. M. L. Stapleton, *Harmful Eloquence: Ovid's Amores from Antiquity to Shakespeare* (Ann Arbor, MI: University of Michigan Press, 1996), 135.
30. Sean Benson, "The Resurrection of the Dead in *The Winter's Tale* and *The Tempest*," *Renascence* 61.1 (Fall 2008): 16.
31. Katherine Heavey, *The Early Modern Medea: Medea in English Literature, 1558–1688* (New York, NY/Basingstoke: Palgrave Macmillan, 2015), 141.
32. *The Tempest*, dir. Julie Taymor (Burbank, CA: Walt Disney Studios Motion Pictures, 2010).
33. Adam Rosenberg (2010), "The Tempest: Julie Taymor Gathers a Perfect Storm," *CBR.com*, October 4, http://www.cbr.com/the-tempest-julie-taymor-gathers-a-perfect-storm/ (last accessed December 12, 2016).
34. Lisa S. Starks-Estes, *Violence, Trauma, and Virtus in Shakespeare's Roman Poems and Plays: Transforming Ovid* (New York, NY: Palgrave Macmillan, 2014), 10.
35. *Prospero's Books*, dir. Peter Greenaway (Santa Monica, CA: Miramax Films, 1991).

CHAPTER 5

1. Samuel Scheffler, "The Afterlife (Part I)," *Death and the Afterlife*, ed. Niko Kolodny (New York, NY/Oxford: Oxford University Press, 2013), 32.
2. Keith Thomas, *The Ends of Life: Roads to Fulfilment in Early Modern England* (Oxford University Press, 2009), 240–1.
3. Richard Crompton, *The Mansion of Magnanimity* (London: Printed [by Richard Field] for William Ponsonby, 1599), A2v.
4. Qtd. in Thomas, *The Ends of Life*, 252. The quotation is drawn from *The Civil Conversation of M. Steeven Guazzo*, trans. George Pettie and Barth. Young (Tudor Translations, 1925), i. 9.
5. Thomas Nashe, *Selected Works*, ed. Stanley Wells (Abingdon/New York, NY: Routledge, 1964), 65.
6. The poems quoted here are all drawn from the "Commendatory Poems and Prefaces" section of the edition of *The Complete Works* used throughout this volume.
7. The trope of the returning ghosts of dead authors was popular in Shakespeare's time, too. Thomas Dekker's *A Knight's Conjuring* (1606) features the ghosts of Christopher Marlowe, George Peele, Edmund Spenser, and Thomas Kyd. Thomas Nashe appears in the anonymous *Tom Nashe His Ghost* (1642). In a variation on the formulation, Thomas Middleton's *Ghost of Lucrece* (1600) summons the figure from both the Roman past and from the pages of Shakespeare's poem to comment upon the tragic events that led to her suicide.

8. Marjorie B. Garber, *Vested Interests: Cross-Dressing and Cultural Anxiety* (London/New York, NY: Routledge, 2011), 33.
9. Garber, *Vested Interest*, 33.
10. Paul Franssen, *Shakespeare's Literary Lives: The Author as Character in Fiction and Film* (Cambridge: Cambridge University Press, 2016), 247.
11. Helen Vendler, *The Art of Shakespeare's Sonnets* (Cambridge/London: Harvard University Press, 1997), 442.
12. Paul Edmondson and Stanley Wells, *Shakespeare's Sonnets* (Oxford: Oxford University Press, 2004), 64.
13. Bacon, *The Major Works*, 343.
14. Bacon, *The Major Works*, 344.
15. The mythical bird appears in another of Shakespeare's poems which dwells upon the theme of the afterlife. In "Let the bird of the loudest lay," the Phoenix, the mythical bird which resurrects from its own ashes, makes an appearance. The poem (sometimes referred to as "The Phoenix and the Turtle") is arguably Shakespeare's most peculiar poem and describes the romantic union and then immolation of a phoenix and her lover, a turtledove. I have omitted it from this study as it (ostensibly) describes non-human participants. If the birds represent historical figures, their identities remain a topic of debate. Michael Dobson and Stanley Wells, the editors of *The Oxford Companion to Shakespeare*, characterize the text as containing Shakespeare's "most cryptic verses." William Shakespeare, *The Oxford Companion to Shakespeare*, eds. Michael Dobson and Stanley Wells (Oxford: Oxford University Press, 2008), 75.
16. Jacques Derrida, *The Politics of Friendship*, trans. George Collins (New York, NY: Verso, 2006), 166–7.
17. Edmondson and Wells, *Shakespeare's Sonnets*, 64.
18. Jacques Derrida, "The Deaths of Roland Barthes," *The Work of Mourning*, eds. Pascale-Anne Brault and Michael Naas (Chicago, IL: University of Chicago Press, 2001), 36.
19. Donne, *Devotions*, 177.
20. Bray, *The Friend*, 65.
21. Mallin, *Godless Shakespeare*, 3.
22. Jacques Derrida, *Politics of Friendship*, 13.
23. This nocturnal place of rest for lost friends maps to the "kingdom of perpetual night" that we hear about in *Richard III*, a figuration that seems to take up the notion of the sleeping soul. The association of death with darkness is a commonplace, and we can hear its roots in the book of Job which describes the afterlife as "Before I go and shall not return, *even* to the land of darkness and shadow of death: Into a land, I *say*, dark as darkness itself, *and* into the shadow of death, where is none order, but the light *is there* as darkness (10:21–2). We can hear resonances of this idea in

John Milton's description of hell in *Paradise Lost* as "shining dark, darkness visible" (1.63). Interestingly, Milton's phrase was used by William Styron to describe his depression in his 1990 biographical work entitled *Darkness Visible: A Memoir of Madness.* The speaker of the sonnets, like so many of the writers and characters we have encountered in this study, imagines the afterlife to be an extreme version of earthly pains or pleasures. In turn, the afterlife offers powerful metaphors for describing our earthly experiences.

24. Phillips, *Side Effects*, 104.
25. Vendler, *The Art of Shakespeare's Sonnets*, 168.
26. Mallin, *Godless Shakespeare*, 3.
27. Scheffler, "The Afterlife (Part I)," 30.
28. Seana Valentine Shiffrin, "Preserving the Valued or Preserving Valuing?," *Death and the Afterlife*, ed. Niko Kolodny (New York, NY/Oxford: Oxford University Press, 2013), 157–8.

Further Reading

There are several, very good studies that broadly consider the afterlife as a concept. Samuel Scheffler approaches the subject by asking a question regarding cultural value: "Whose afterlives matter more?" His discussion, in *Death and the Afterlife* (Oxford University Press, 2016), concludes that it matters more that humanity proceeds us than that our own personal lives are prolonged. Carlos Eire's wonderful and insightful *A Very Brief History of Eternity* (Princeton University Press, 2010) explores the very notion of eternity across cultures and across time periods. Other broad but useful studies trace the history of changing conceptions of the afterlife. These include Mario Erasmo's *Death: Antiquity and Its Legacy* (I.B. Tauris & Co Ltd, 2012), which examines traditions regarding death and burial in ancient Greece and Rome before noting how they have changed over time. In *After Lives: A Guide to Heaven, Hell, and Purgatory* (Oxford University Press, 2009), John Casey provides a substantive history of changing ideas about life after death in the Christian tradition. Two other, general studies in the same vein are *Beyond Death: Theological and Philosophical Reflections on Life after Death*, eds. Dan Cohn-Sherbok and Christopher Lewis (Palgrave MacMillan, 1995) and Alan F. Segal's *Life After Death: A History of the Afterlife in Western Religion* (Doubleday, 2004).

Several studies look specifically at the peculiar history of the concept of Purgatory. Readers of the present volume may want to start with Stephen Greenblatt's *Hamlet in Purgatory* (Princeton University Press, 2001), which scrutinizes Purgatory as a space forbidden by sixteenth-century English authority yet thrust into the audience's imagination by the ghost of Hamlet's father. Elizabeth Tingle's *Purgatory and Piety in Brittany 1480–1720* (Routledge, 2016), D. P. Walker's *The Decline of Hell: Seventeenth-Century Discussions of Eternal Torment* (University of Chicago Press, 1964), and Jacques Le Goff's *The Birth of Purgatory* (University of Chicago Press, 1986) further explore the convoluted understandings of Purgatory within medieval and Renaissance theological and cultural discourses.

Turning our attention to cultural beliefs in England, two useful resources are Frederick M. Keener's *English Dialogues of the Dead: A Critical History, an Anthology, and a Check List* (Columbia University Press, 1973) and Carol Zaleski's *Otherworld Journeys: Accounts of Near-Death Experiences in Medieval and Modern Times* (Oxford University Press, 1987), which enters the discussion of supernatural experience by delving into near-death narratives through different historical lenses and consideration of skeptics and near-death experience researchers alike. Piero Camporesi specifically looks at the culture's polarizing imagery of hell and the eucharist in *Fear of Hell: Images of Damnation and Salvation in Early Modern Europe* (Pennsylvania State University Press, 1991). Keith Thomas' *Religion and the Decline of Magic: Studies in Popular Beliefs in Sixteenth and Seventeenth-Century England* (Oxford University Press, 1971) examines how magic intermingled with early modern English religious beliefs. Philip C. Almond's *Heaven and Hell in Enlightenment England* (Cambridge University Press, 1994) aids in drawing a genealogy of beliefs just beyond Shakespeare's time as it looks at beliefs during the period 1650–1750.

For those seeking to understand how death and the afterlife were depicted on stage by Shakespeare's contemporaries, two studies stand out as helpful starting points. Michael Neill's *Issues of Death: Mortality and Identity in English Renaissance Tragedy* (Oxford University Press, 1997) locates tragedies by Shakespeare and his contemporaries in relation to conceptions of death in the Renaissance cultural imagination. William Engel's *Death and Drama in Renaissance England: Shades of Memory* (Oxford University Press, 2003) similarly tracks death as a crucial element in the narrative of tragedy and offers interesting discussion of emblems as a means by which the dead were memorialized by the living. Robert N. Watson's *The Rest is Silence: Death as Annihilation in the English Renaissance* (University of California Press, 1995) renders visible the impulse to rebel against mortality in Renaissance cultural depictions, discussing *Hamlet*, *Measure for Measure*, and *Macbeth*. Ramie Targoff's *Posthumous Love: Eros and the Afterlife in Renaissance England* (University of Chicago Press, 2014) specifically elucidates how early modern writing sought to resist the mortal nature of love and fantasize about reunion after death in such texts as *Romeo and Juliet*. Those interested in cultural debates about whether couples reunite after death will find useful essays in *Love after Death: Concepts of Posthumous Love in Medieval and Early Modern Europe*, edited by Bernhard Jussen and Ramie Targoff (De Gruyter, 2015). The volume offers examples of posthumous lovers from classical antiquity through the Renaissance and traces debates about the likelihood of reunion in England and on the continent. Readers interested in the larger interplay between sex and death will want to begin with Georges Bataille's foundational *Erotism: Death and Sensuality* (City Lights Books, 1986).

Placing focus on memorialization, several volumes help us understand how writing about the dead—whether on the page or on the funeral monument—falls into the larger realm of literary study. These include Scott Newstok's *Quoting Death in Early Modern England: The Poetics of Epitaphs Beyond the Tomb* (Palgrave Macmillan, 2009) and Joshua Scodel's *The English Poetic Epitaph: Commemoration and Conflict from Jonson to Wordsworth* (Cornell University Press, 1991). Armando Petrucci traces the tradition and function of funerary writing in *Writing the Dead: Death and Writing Strategies in the Western Tradition* (Stanford University Press, 1998). *Time's Purpled Masquers: Stars and the Afterlife in Renaissance English Literature* by Alastair Fowler (Clarendon Press, 1996) chronicles the Renaissance culture's astronomical beliefs about the afterlife and considers how these informed literary celebrations of deceased writers. William E. Engel's *Mapping Mortality: The Persistence of Memory and Melancholy in Early Modern England* (University of Massachusetts Press, 1995) includes discussion of writing but goes beyond it to examine painting and other forms of visual art. Two recent studies highlight the role of material culture in linking the living and the dead. Nigel Llewellyn's *Funeral Monuments in Post-Reformation England* (Cambridge University Press, 2009) focuses on the carved stone funeral monument. This is the first comprehensive modern account of English monuments to the dead and complements Peter Shylock's *Monuments and Memory in Early Modern England* (Ashgate, 2008), which interprets the visual iconography of such monuments. Both help set the cultural context for the ways in which Shakespeare's audience may have interpreted scenes depicting how the dead are laid to rest or what mementos are used to remember those that have passed.

Funeral elegies in early modern England have been the object of several interesting studies, including those by Dennis Kay, G. W. Pigman, and Peter Sacks. With *Melodious Tears: The English Funeral Elegy from Spenser to Milton* (Oxford University Press, 1990), Kay provides a useful overview of the tropes at work across major works in the elegiac genre. In *Grief and English Renaissance Elegy* (Cambridge University Press, 1985), Pigman takes a psychoanalytic approach to help us see the different ways that love is connected to mourning, especially in early modern poetic expressions that involve idealization of the mourned individual and an expression of need for consoling by the mourner. Sacks calls attention to how the work of mourning involves a deflection of desire, as the mourner must accept the loss of the beloved and prepare to redirect affection towards another in the future in *The English Elegy: Studies in the Genre from Spenser to Yeats* (John Hopkins University Press, 1985). Two important complements to these studies are Diana Fuss's *Dying Modern: A Meditation on Elegy* (Duke University Press, 2013) and Melissa F. Zeiger's *Beyond Consolation: Death, Sexuality, and the Changing Shapes of Elegy* (Cornell University Press, 1997), both of which consider modern implications of funeral elegy while also remaining cognizant of its early roots.

Any discussion of remembrance and the way that the living relate to the dead inevitably leads one into the burgeoning field of early modern memory studies. Broad studies of the significance of memory in Renaissance literature, including useful discussion of how the dead bear upon the living, are Kyle Pivetti's *Of Memory and Literary Form: Making the Early Modern English Nation* (University of Delaware Press, 2015) and Andrew Hiscock's *Reading*

Memory in Early Modern Literature (Cambridge University Press, 2011). Both emphasize the important distinction between personal memory and collective memory as individuals and groups situate themselves in relation to those that lived in the past. Readers who are interested in pursuing the theme of memory in Shakespeare will find Hester Lees-Jeffries' comprehensive examination in *Shakespeare and Memory* (Oxford University Press, 2013) to be an excellent resource. Jonathan Baldo's *Memory in Shakespeare's Histories: Stages of Forgetting in Early Modern England* (Routledge, 2012) will also be a helpful resource for tracing this theme. Three insightful studies that consider how the dynamics of memory relate to Shakespearean performance are Garrett A. Sullivan Jr.'s *Memory and Forgetting in English Renaissance Drama: Shakespeare, Marlowe, and Webster* (Cambridge University Press, 2005); the volume *Shakespeare: Memory and Performance*, ed. Peter Holland (Cambridge University Press, 2006); and Lina Perkins Wilder's *Shakespeare's Memory Theatre: Recollection, Properties, and Character* (Cambridge University Press, 2010).

The treatment of the dead and attitudes towards what happens after death in early modern English culture are elaborated on in several volumes, including Keith Thomas' *The Ends of Life: Roads to Fulfilment in Early Modern England* (Oxford University Press, 2009) which offers a short chapter on notions of the afterlife and suggests that personal fame in the living world offered a compelling strategy for those seeking a way to continue living in the physical world after death. *Dying, Death, Burial, and Commemoration in Reformation Europe*, eds. Elizabeth Tingle and Jonathan Willis (Routledge, 2014) and Vanessa Harding's *The Dead and Living in Paris and London, 1500–1670* (Cambridge University Press, 2002) both offer insight on burial and other funeral practices of the period. *The Place of the Dead: Death and Remembrance in Late Medieval and Early Modern Europe*, eds. Bruce Gordon and Peter Marshall (Cambridge University Press, 2000), explores how these practices reflected early modern social attitudes and concerns. Joseph Roach's *Cities of the Dead: Circum-Atlantic Performance* (Columbia University Press, 1996) examines death and burial practices through the lens of cultural exchange as he takes the Mardi Gras Indians as an intriguing starting point for his analysis. Douglas Trevor writes about the emotions and relationships that drive grief and mourning throughout early modern writing in *The Poetics of Melancholy in Early Modern England* (Cambridge University Press, 2004).

Early modern understandings of death and the afterlife were further complicated by their shifting viewpoints on suicide. *From Sin to Insanity*, ed. Jeffrey R. Watt (Cornell University Press, 2004), offers an extensive consideration of the elements—including legal and social perspectives—that influenced how early modern European culture viewed self-murder. Michael MacDonald and Terence R. Murphy's *Sleepless Souls: Suicide in Early Modern England* (Clarendon Press, 1991) looks at early modern England specifically.

R. A. Houston's *Punishing the Dead?: Suicide, Lordship, and Community in Britain, 1500–1830* (Oxford University Press, 2010) also offers a useful focus on England but with an overview on a longer historical period.

Some very interesting work has been done regarding early modern beliefs, especially as they pertain to those figures that cross the boundary between the living and the dead. For example, Kristen Poole's *Supernatural Environments in Shakespeare's England: Spaces of Demonism, Divinity, and Drama* (Cambridge University Press, 2011), discusses those earthly spaces in which humans might encounter some vision of the world beyond that of the living, mentioning *Othello*, *Hamlet*, *Macbeth*, and *The Tempest*. Two recent collections feature work that helps inform the context for how various supernatural entities might be understood by Shakespeare's audience: *The Extraordinary and the Everyday in Early Modern England*, eds. Garthine Walker and Angela McShane-Jones (Palgrave, 2010) and *Supernatural and Secular Power*, eds. Marcus Harmes and Victoria Bladen (Ashgate, 2015). Two volumes that help us understand the figure of the demon in early modern England are John D. Cox's exploration of stage depictions in *The Devil and the Sacred in English Drama, 1350–1642* (Cambridge University Press, 2000) and Ewan Fernie's broader study of the figure in *The Demonic: Literature and Experience* (Routledge, 2013). Cynthia Marshall's *Last Things and Last Plays: Shakespearean Eschatology* (Southern Illinois University Press, 1991) looks specifically at four plays—*Cymbeline*, *Pericles*, *The Winter's Tale*, and *The Tempest*—to explore the themes of death, judgment, and afterlife within the context of early modern beliefs. Sean Benson's *Shakespearean Resurrection: The Art of Almost Raising the Dead* (Duquesne University Press, 2009) traces Shakespeare's interest in theatrical resurrection.

As we have seen in this book, ghosts frequent early modern literature. Several broad studies help us think through the nature of the phantom, and many of these are influenced by "hauntology," or the theorization of the spectral, as introduced by Jacques Derrida in *Spectres of Marx* (Routledge, 1994). Key studies include *Ghosts: Deconstruction, Psychoanalysis, History*, eds. Peter Buse and Andrew Stott (Macmillan, 1999), which tracks haunting through literature, and Marvin Carlson's *The Haunted Stage* (University of Michigan Press, 2001), which looks at the figurative ghosts of theater that remind spectators of what they have already seen. Avery Gordon's *Ghostly Matters: Haunting and the Sociological Imagination* (University of Minnesota Press, 2008) considers how the ghost offers a useful heuristic device for manifesting how deceased members of a community who formerly wielded dominant social power still influence the living in terms of preconceptions of gender, class, and race. Leo Braudy's *Haunted: On Ghosts, Witches, Vampires, Zombies, and Other Monsters of the Natural and Supernatural Worlds* (Yale University Press, 2016) examines representations of supernatural entities, including ghosts, from the Reformation to pop culture.

The role of religion in Shakespeare's work has been the object of numerous studies. I highlight here several volumes that provide useful starting points, especially for readers desiring to better understand how early modern religious belief informs depictions of characters and moral questions in the plays. David Scott Kastan describes the function of religion throughout Shakespeare's work in *A Will to Believe: Shakespeare and Religion* (Oxford University Press, 2014). *Spiritual Shakespeares*, ed. Ewan Fernie (Routledge, 2005), contains essays that examine religious belief from a presentist perspective. Eric S. Mallin's *Godless Shakespeare* (Continuum, 2007) finds Shakespeare's characters exhibiting skepticism and unbelief rather than the pious beliefs popularized by his time. Shakespeare's work plays an important role in several incisive studies of the interplay between affective expression and personal belief in early modern theater. Steven Mullaney's *The Reformation of Emotions in the Age of Shakespeare* (University of Chicago Press, 2015) describes how theater in the Renaissance offered an arena in which writers and audiences could process the emotions associated with social change, while Susan Zimmerman looks specifically about how the dead body on stage offered a focal point for projecting anxieties about dying and changing attitudes about death in *The Early Modern Corpse and Shakespeare's Theatre* (Edinburgh University Press, 2005). Donovan Sherman's *Second Death: Theatricalities of the Soul in Shakespeare's Drama* (Edinburgh University Press, 2016) goes as far as to claim the soul as a theatrical concept, looking at *The Merchant of Venice*, *The Winter's Tale*, and *Coriolanus*.

Another way of thinking about the intersection between Shakespeare and the afterlife would be to think about how his work has had lasting effects on language, and expressions of this have at times framed Shakespeare as a ghost-figure himself. Marjorie Garber's *Shakespeare's Ghost Writers: Literature as Uncanny Causality* (Routledge, 1987) explores Shakespeare as if he himself were a ghost—where ghostwriters could have been involved in his work and he a missing figure. Continuing to examine the figure of Shakespeare after his death, Michael Dobson's *The Making of the National Poet: Shakespeare, Adaption, and Authorship, 1660–1769* (Clarendon Press, 1995) offers very interesting discussion about Shakespeare's appearance as a ghost in several plays who authorizes adaptations of his work. An excellent complement to Dobson's study is the recent collection *Canonising Shakespeare: Stationers and the Book Trade, 1640–1740*, eds. Emma Depledge and Peter Kirwan (Cambridge University Press, 2017), which offers fresh insight into the role of printers, editors, and booksellers in shaping Shakespeare's place in the canon and authorial identity. Paul Franssen's *Shakespeare's Literary Lives: The Author as Character in Fiction and Film* (Cambridge University Press, 2016) explores the playwright's posthumous appearances in drama, poetry, and fiction.

Index

The manufacturer's authorised representative in the EU for product safety is Oxford University Press España S.A. of el Parque Empresarial San Fernando de Henares, Avenida de Castilla, 2 – 28830 Madrid (www.oup.es/en or product.safety@oup.com). OUP España S.A. also acts as importer into Spain of products made by the manufacturer.

www.ingramcontent.com/pod-product-compliance
Ingram Content Group UK Ltd.
Pitfield, Milton Keynes, MK11 3LW, UK
UKHW020226250726
13967UKWH00001B/216

* 9 7 8 0 1 9 8 8 0 1 1 0 8 *